CHRIST IN A PONCHO

Testimonials of the Nonviolent Struggles
in Latin America

ADOLFO PÉREZ ESQUIVEL

Edited by Charles Antoine

Translated from the French by Robert R. Barr

ORBIS BOOKS
Maryknoll, New York 10545

The Catholic Foreign Mission Society of America (Maryknoll) recruits and trains people for overseas missionary service. Through Orbis Books Maryknoll aims to foster the international dialogue that is essential to mission. The books published, however, reflect the opinions of their authors and are not meant to represent the official position of the society.

First published as *Le Christ au poncho, suivi de témoignages de luttes non-violentes en Amérique Latine,* edited and translated by Charles Antoine with the collaboration of Michel Grolleaud, Pierre Olhagaray, and Michel Piton, copyright © Editions du Centurion, 1981, 17, rue de Babylone, 75007 Paris.

English translation © 1983 by Orbis Books, Maryknoll, NY 10545.
Manufactured in the United States of America

Manuscript editor: Robert J. Cunningham

Library of Congress Cataloging in Publication Data

Pérez Esquivel, Adolfo.
Christ in a poncho.

   Translation of: Le Christ au poncho.
   Includes bibliographical references.
   1. Nonviolence—Religious aspects—Christianity.
2. Latin America—Politics and government—
1948–   . I. Title.
BT736.6.P4713   1982   261.7'098   82-18760
ISBN 0-88344-104-7 (pbk.)

Contents

Introduction

Words flashed over the teletypes on October 13, 1980: "Nobel Peace Prize has been awarded to Adolfo Pérez Esquivel."

Who? Newsrooms bustled with confusion. Little by little the disconcerting truth dawned. Adolfo Pérez Esquivel was unknown to the media.*

Pérez was certainly less than altogether familiar to the Norwegian paper that started out its story with the casual observation that he was a Brazilian. That error was quickly corrected (not quickly enough to keep it from being copied worldwide, however)—only to have an Argentine radio station hypothesize that he was from Paraguay. Eventually the elusive identity began to emerge. Adolfo Pérez Esquivel was an Argentinean—a disciple of Gandhi and an advocate of nonviolence—and this was why he had received the Nobel Prize.

Latin America in Pain and Travail

Adolfo Pérez Esquivel is a man of about fifty, with thick brown hair (above a receding hairline) and an altogether tranquil mien. He is a painter and sculptor by profession. His movements and gestures are measured. He is a keen observer, and an earnest contemplator of what he has observed.

Without a doubt the first thing that strikes you about Pérez is the way he looks at you through his large, dark-rimmed glasses. You are his friend. His brown eyes gaze out at you from the depths of his person. He has a habit of regarding other persons and things with tenderness and penetration. His face is just right for

---

*According to Spanish-language custom, the full name consists of the Christian name, the surname "Pérez," and the mother's family name "Esquivel."

1

television—you can see the serenity there, behind the lines life has etched.

This Buenos Aires native talks very little about himself. He lost his mother when he was three. Later we find him in a Catholic boarding school. They used to call him a difficult child. (You might şay that. Little Adolfo was independent. He took care of himself—with his fists.) He was a stubborn worker, determined to "go it alone." He worked his way through Fine Arts in college.

Pérez Esquivel is a little bit more voluble about his family. He has received so much from them, he says. His wife, Amanda (her middle name is Itati—there is some Guaraní blood there), is a pianist and composer. Their three sons, Leonardo, Victor Ernesto, and Esteban, range in age from fifteen to twenty-five. The eldest is already following in his father's footsteps, and heads up the Argentine office of the Latin American Nonviolence Movement.

But what Pérez really likes to talk about is what he has been doing for the past ten years from one end of Latin America to the other. Through the Peace and Justice Service, his brainchild, he coordinates the activities of a variety of groups fighting for peace, justice, and human rights.

The Nobel Prize, says Adolfo over and over again, reaches far beyond his simple person. The Nobel Peace Prize for 1980 goes to all his brothers and sisters in Latin America—especially to the poorest and the most oppressed, and to the hundreds and thousands of nameless women and men who are battling for the dignity of the humble and fighting for respect for the ones they call the "marginalized"—the little people whom economic growth has passed right by: peasants robbed of their land; Indians scorned by modern society; the forgotten inhabitants of sprawling suburbs or shantytowns; Bolivian miners' wives; workers fired in São Paulo or Mexico City because they dared to strike; and the mothers of the fifteen thousand young people "missing" in Argentina today. A whole Latin America wells up in your heart to hear him—a Latin America in anguish and agony. But it is a Latin America full of hope, too, and already winning victories.

Adolfo Pérez Esquivel is a latecomer to nonviolence. He was forty years old—this Master of Arts at Buenos Aires and La

Plata, this sculpture teacher—when he discovered nonviolent action. It was the fruit of a long journey. As a teenager, Adolfo had read about those "masters of action" Gandhi and Martin Luther King, Jr. But for the intuition to take flesh he had to meet up with Lanza del Vasto and with Jean and Hildegard Goss-Mayr of the International Fellowship of Reconciliation. So many elements contributed to the gradual molding of the thought and action of this new militant! Now the artist entered his "time of incarnation and conversion," as he likes to put it, and even his sculptural works began to take on the form of a suffering America.

For some years the painter and sculptor in Adolfo had felt the need to "find my American roots," and "get a direct experience of the pre-Columbian cultures." His encounter with nonviolence only hastened his plunge into the ancient Indian civilizations of the continent. This experience, in turn, sparked an awareness of the extent of today's injustice whose victims, by design, are the Indians of the Andes and the Amazon rain forest. And so it came about that drawing and painting led Adolfo off on the "long pilgrimage of the peoples in quest of their own liberation."

The Generals' Argentina

It is not a matter of indifference that the nonviolent Adolfo Pérez Esquivel is an Argentinean. His personal development is doubtless partially bound up with the climate of social and political violence that has scarred his country for nearly a decade and a half.

In 1969 Argentinean society was shaken by an outburst of violence whose seriousness and depth would only come to light in the following years. In May and June of that year, the Córdoba riots occurred, pitting students and workers against the forces of General Juan Carlos Ongania, and costing a number of deaths among the rioters. The *cordobazo,* as these events came to be called, was only the visible tip of a deep, growing agitation among Argentine youth. Their boiling spirits and hopes for social change would only intensify over the next years, and General Ongania would be unequal to events. Following his coup in 1966, Ongania had thought to model his Argentine revolution on the pattern of the Brazilian generals who had invented the National Security Doctrine. But Ongania was overthrown by General Roberto Levingston, and Levingston was deposed in March 1971 by General Alejandro Lanusse. Now the guerrilla war, the direct result of the *cordobazo,* became much more spectacularly violent. Grafted onto an authoritarian political approach and neoliberal type economy, the political violence of the Montoneros and of the People's Revolutionary Army (the ERP) was on fertile ground—the waxing discontent of the popular classes, who had been dealt such a heavy blow by the plummeting quality of life.

"Who runs things in Argentina?" asked a Buenos Aires journalist in 1972. "Fear," he was told. Fear indeed. In a like climate, the army naturally meant to stay in control. And the internal war against subversive movements began.

But now General Lanusse had to reckon with that gigantic figure of the Argentinean scene, former President Juan Perón. In disgrace since 1955 and all but forgotten in his Madrid retreat, Perón had only been awaiting the propitious moment to return to the front page. "The vast majority of the people were, and are, Peronists," it was said. This was a historical fact. Now it came into the game as the opposition's trump card. Workers' organizations especially—that central political force on the Argentine chessboard—hailed the return of the Leader. Even the guerrilla movements, for the most part, rallied to Perón. The ex-president became the de facto arbiter of the whole political situation in his country. After a long and stubborn silence punctuated by contradictory statements that muddled things, Juan Perón returned to Argentina for good. On September 23, 1973, he was elected president of the Republic once more—triumphantly, with 61 percent of the vote, and his wife, Isabelita, as vice-president.

But for the Perón myth it was the beginning of the end. Luckily for the Great Leader, he died the following year. Isabelita took over the presidency, and by a rare paradox of politics (largely due to the influence of her adviser and minister, José López Rega), "La Presidente" managed for all practical purposes to destroy Peronism in Argentina.

Back in the barracks, the military were only awaiting the right moment. On March 24, 1976, they returned to the political scene with a vengeance. Lt. Gen. Jorge Rafael Videla's coup marked the definitive beginning of the era of National Security, the "dirty war" against subversion whose implacability has become notorious.

An *"Intolerable Affront"*

In a statement on the antisubversive activity of the Argentinean armed forces, General Riveros could blithely declare to members of the Organization of American States meeting in Washington in January 1980:

We waged this war with our orders in hand, straight from the high command. All false accusations to the contrary, we never had need of any paramilitary organization. We had the military capacity and the legal organization to combat these irregulars quite adequately, however unconventional the war they may have been waging against us. We won, and they won't forgive us. They tell us we violated human rights. Personally I don't see how. In a war like that you have to fight, just as in any other war. Planes don't drop flowers, or the Civil Code, or the Charter of the Rights of Man in a conventional war. When tanks are coming at you, you don't flag them down with a text of Roman jurisprudence. This was war, a subversive, revolutionary war, and the terrorists were themselves using all the means of terror they had at their disposal, every weapon possible. Anybody who thinks he's going to defend himself with roses in that kind of war has already lost it. And then the pro-Communist outfits launch their cute counteroffensive in the form of a cry for the "return of the missing persons," and reproach the Argentine government with "unorthodox methods of combat." Against delinquents like that? This is simple—or studied—ignorance. Our critics ignore the fact that it was the generals and admirals who conducted our war—not a dictator or a dictatorship, as they try to make the international community believe. That war was conducted by a military junta of my country through the intermediary of the Joint Chiefs of Staff.[1]

One could scarcely have wished for a better summary of the state of the problem from the viewpoint of the Argentine military. Imagine their stupefaction, then, when they learned that the Nobel Peace Prize for 1980 had been awarded to an Argentine national who publicly questioned the basic principles and methods of their repressive style of politics!

The General Staff officers of the Buenos Aires junta straightforwardly protected the Nobel Committee's "intolerable affront" to their national dignity. Somewhat more cautiously, governmental circles registered a "surprise on the part of our national public opinion," insisting in a long communiqué that there was no way to make a valid judgment of the politics of the military junta without taking into account the state of war that had obtained in the country since 1969.

Of course, what actually placed General Videla's government in such a poor light was that it had arrested and tortured the future Nobel laureate, and then imprisoned him for fourteen months without trial or even judicial disposition. No one was fooled by the Argentine government's tardy protest in October 1980:

> The activity engaged in by the architect Pérez Esquivel as our country was caught up in the peak intensity of an armed struggle against terrorism, was, against his own intentions, put to use by others to secure the impunity of members of various terrorist groups. Hence he had to be arrested and placed at the disposal of the national executive power—in conformity with the norms in effect during a state of siege. When the fighting abated, he was freed by decision of the national executive power.[2]

Pilgrim of Nonviolence

Adolfo Pérez Esquivel's prison experience became an integral part of his militancy, if only by way of corollary. From this moment forward, the future Nobel laureate plied the length and breadth of Latin America, supporting, assisting, and coordinating the various activities being carried on in most of the countries of Central and South America.

Pérez attended meetings of the nonviolent liberation movement in Costa Rica in 1971 and Colombia in 1974. This movement was concerned with adopting the intellectual tradition of nonviolence and pacificism received from Europe and the United States, but it paid equal attention to the popular character of the movement in Latin America: "It is the poor who are the agents of nonviolent liberation." It was on this occasion that Adolfo Pérez Esquivel was entrusted with the direction of the continental secretariat of the Service for Latin American Nonviolent Activity, whose headquarters was established in Buenos Aires. The *Peace and Justice* bulletin founded by Adolfo in 1973 became its official organ.

In 1974 we find Pérez Esquivel in Ecuador at the side of the peasants of Llangahua and Toctezinín, who were locked in a struggle against the large landowners. In Bolivia he supported the amnesty movement. In Argentina he built an organization of young people whose aim was to encourage the episcopate of that country to take a position in the climate of political degradation into which his native land was fast sinking. In 1975 he went to Paraguay to visit the Christian communities of the Peasant Leagues that were struggling to survive a vicious repression. He went to Brazil to set up a meeting on nonviolence for the Latin American bishops—and to help free a militant Brazilian peasant—and was arrested briefly by military authorities in São Paulo. He went to Honduras in Central America to lend his support to the National Peasant Union. In Argentina itself he took part in the creation of the Permanent Human Rights Assembly, and then the following year in the establishment of the Ecumenical Human Rights Movement.

In 1976 Pérez undertook a long pilgrimage across all Latin America, the Caribbean, North America, and Europe. On his return, as he was passing through Ecuador, he was arrested along with seventeen Latin American bishops at a meeting with Bishop Leonidas Proaño of Riobamba and expelled from the country.

Back in Argentina once more, Adolfo was arrested on April 4, 1977, and "placed at the disposition of the executive branch." This means that he was jailed. And jailed he stayed without indictment, until June 22, 1978, when he was released from detention but placed under house arrest for fourteen more months.

Finally he was free—and he took up his pilgrim's staff of non-violence and started criss-crossing Latin America all over again.

A Whole Mosaic of Experiences

Unlike Gandhi or King, Pérez Esquivel is not a charismatic figure who can take charge of a popular movement and brand it with a spellbinding personality. Adolfo is basically a coordinator of projects already under way and of movements that for the most part were begun without his direct collaboration.

"We try to bring different groups into contact with one another—to set up a tradeoff of experiences and to get them to support one another," he writes. This was his purpose in creating the Service for Nonviolent Activity in Latin America. In the liberation movement of this sprawling region the first thing that needs to be done is to create channels of communication among the many groups and movements carrying out nonviolent struggles nearly everywhere. Often these movements are not even consciously aware of being nonviolent in the technical sense. But this is no matter. What matters is to get them all coordinated.

Next, pressure must be brought to bear on governments. "Once we've laid the foundations," Adolfo goes on, "the next thing is to witness—to denounce prophetically the situations of injustice in which peasants, workers, and religious groups have to live." To judge by the repression encountered by these social groups, it cannot exactly be claimed that the governmental authorities are indifferent to the pressures such groups bring to bear in their peaceful battle for their rights.

The task of prophetic denunciation was to grow to imposing proportions. Patiently and doggedly Pérez Esquivel wove the fabric of what would one day become a genuine popular movement. Soon it would join the Brazilian laborers at the Perús cement factory in São Paulo, the Ecuadorian Indians of Riobamba, the peasants of the Paraguayan Agrarian Leagues, the mothers and fathers of young people who had disappeared in Argentina, the peasants of the Alagamar plantation in Brazil's Northeast, the miners' wives in Bolivia, and the field workers of the Solidarity Vicariate in Santiago, Chile. How many separate, different experiences! Yet all displayed the badge of combat for justice and a nonviolence that appealed to existing law.

It is easy to see that there is a mighty nonviolent movement afoot in Latin America. In this book the reader will have a glimpse of some of its most urgent struggles.

A first mark of Latin American nonviolence, then, is the multiplicity and variety of its experiences. A second is its close ties with the Catholic hierarchy.

Let us make it quite clear from the outset that we do not mean that the church has taken over the nonviolent movement in Latin America. In fact, if we look at the number of bishops who actually mistrust it—beginning with those in Argentina, Adolfo's own country—we could just as well speak of the church's rejection of the movement. But certain bishops play a front-line role in the battle for social justice. Best known are Dom Hélder Câmara, Bishop Antônio Fragoso, Cardinal Paulo Evaristo Arns of São Paulo, and Archbishop José Pires. But there are also Bishops Leonidas Proaño in Ecuador, Samuel Ruiz in Mexico, and Fernando Ariztía in Chile. And is there anyone, anywhere, who does not know of Oscar Romero, the archbishop of San Salvador, who was murdered for asking the soldiers to stop killing their peasant sisters and brothers?

It was at a meeting of a score of bishops in Bogotá, Colombia, in 1977 that the foundations of a veritable charter of nonviolence in Latin America were laid. Addressed to the Christian communities of the continent, the meeting's final document sets forth a series of considerations on "evangelical nonviolence as a force for liberation." We append the complete text of this statement at the end of this book.

Sons and Daughters of Medellín

Thus it came about that nonviolence in Latin America built its edifice at the confluence of two mighty torrents, both of them immense in their tributaries: the militarization of power, which strains unjust social relationships to the breaking point on the pretext of economic development and "national security," and the evolution of the church, which, through certain of its bishops, is taking the measure of "gospel radicalism" as it steps up its fight for the dignity of the poor of Latin America.

The church passed the point of no return in 1968. The occasion was the Second General Conference of the Latin American

Bishops at Medellín in Peru. "We are all the children of Medellín," Adolfo loves to say to the Christians of Latin America. This means that all Latin American efforts of Christian renewal and all Latin American Christian projects in the battle for justice today have their foundation and justification in what the Medellín Conference declared in 1968. Medellín is the very source and spring of the living waters of Latin American non-violence.

It is scarcely accidental, then, that the green hope of Pérez Esquivel's activity should take root in Christian soil.

On one of his first trips to Ecuador, Adolfo had a dream one night. He dreamed he saw Christ on the cross—wearing an Indian poncho. Some days later, not far from Riobamba he stood riveted before a crucifix in the humble little chapel of a community of the Little Brothers of Charles de Foucauld. There it was on the wall again: Christ in a poncho. An artist did not need much more. Adolfo painted the scene we have on our back cover.

Fruit of a dream dawning in the Andes among Indians (a dream whose long ripening took place in the jails of the Argentine), *Christ in a Poncho* marks the end of a long, slow stage in the spiritual evolution of one human being and a step in his pilgrimage of self-liberation. If faith may be defined as the interior dimension of a historical experience lived in the context of one national tragedy after another, then Pérez Esquivel must be a great believer.

In La Plata Prison Adolfo was forbidden all books, even a Bible. Faced with long days and nights of solitude he had time to appreciate what he calls "God's silence"—the place where faith ripens. Here in prison, everything Adolfo had ever received in the way of Christian culture began to come back to him in an uninterrupted series of insights, at once familiar and fresh. A kind of spiritual nourishment took charge, and Adolfo found, for instance, that he could write out whole passages of the gospel by heart. Once more in the history of oppression, for Adolfo as for so many before and after him, the lethal experience of prison paradoxically became an experience of interior liberation—a kind of spiritual striking root.

Now two mighty ideas ranged themselves as the forefront of Adolfo's permanent concerns. First, he was struck by the need

Christians have to experience a church that is poor and pro-phetic—the basic inspiration of the Medellín Conference. The Christian experience of life, in its most authentic Latin American expression today, is based on (1) the ancestral call to poverty as ascesis and as availability to others; (2) propheticism as a social dimension of divine revelation; and (3) witness as the expression of solidarity in human nature with the victims of oppression, whether we find these victims in some particular society or flung across a whole region.

Adolfo's second key idea is the simple fact of the "effectiveness of the ineffective." Adolfo's heroes are John the Baptist, the Forerunner, the one who said he would have to become small in order for the Other to appear in his full stature; Charles de Foucauld, the towering spiritual master of abandonment into the Father's hands; Gandhi and King, those giants of nonviolence who were so effective because Transcendence dwelt within them; Thomas Merton, the North American who became a monk, and then converted the Nicaraguan poet Ernesto Cardenal; Saint Francis of Assisi, the Poverello who said, "Make me an artisan of Your peace," and then proceeded to exalt the world on the lever of his nakedness; and—least "effective" of all—Christ, the One whose ignominious death gave the signal for the resurrection from the dead of all who believe in the power of the Name.

A Light Shining in the Darkness

On the occasion of the solemn conferral of the Nobel Peace Prize, in Oslo on December 10, 1980, John Sanness, president of the Nobel Committee, said this of Adolfo Pérez Esquivel:

> For years he has dedicated himself to the cause of human rights in Argentina and in all Latin America. He is a per-suaded messenger of the principle of nonviolence in the po-litical and social battle for emancipation. He has lighted a light in the darkness. The committee is of the view that that light ought to be kept burning.

How could anyone not subscribe to this resolution when hu-man beings on this planet are threatened in their very existence by violence—a violence all reasoned out and coldly planned?

Latin America is writing a saga in fire and blood. It is the saga of the Christ-sign—the Christ of the poor. It is the saga of the gospel—the gospel in its stark nakedness and irresistible power. It is the saga of the gospel as lived today from Peru's lofty plateau to the Brazilian littoral, and from Mexico's volcanos to the pampas of the Argentine. It is the saga of the Beatitudes—for at this very moment, as the reader's eyes move along these lines, the heart-beats of dozens of millions of the humble people of the earth, grown anxious for a liberation that is too long in coming, are preparing to strike a chord of hope and faith and glory. For blessed are the poor.

Charles Antoine

PART ONE

The Ant and the Elephant:
The Voice of Adolfo Pérez Esquivel

*"True, the elephant is stronger. But the ants . . . well, there are
more of them."*

*Adolfo Pérez Esquivel's analogy for his battle for peace and
justice shows the odds in their true proportions.*

*But what inspires nonviolence? What is it built on? How is its
original insight "concretized"—in other words, what are its avenues to action? And what are the nature and limits of that action?
Here are Adolfo's answers.*

*The prison experience is part and parcel of the struggle for the
dignity of the little people of Latin America. Adolfo was given no
dispensation from this rule. He too has learned in his flesh the
truth of Emmanuel Mounier's awesome pronouncement: "It is a
deprivation for a person not to have known illness, misfortune, or
prison." In the people's democracies of the East it is only logical
for people to go to jail for militancy on behalf of human rights.
Freedom of conscience is the only liberty that does not lie pros-
trate at the feet of state control. But how paradoxical that in Latin
America it is the "defense of western Christian civilization" that
confers on the military the power to arrest, torture, and even murder the witnesses of the gospel. Yet this is the simple fact. Adolfo's
experience is no different from that of thousands upon thousands*

*of other Latin Americans. But behold, they emerge more pure
and strong than before!*

*But now to the ant . . . and to his testimony that was recorded
in December 1980.*

When did I decide for nonviolent combat?

It's hard to say. Everybody takes on his or her commitments gradually. When I was a teen-ager, I read all sorts of books, good ones, bad ones—excellent ones, some of them, like Gandhi's autobiography, Thomas Merton's works (which I still read regularly), and the books by Père René Voillaume of the Little Brothers of Jesus, the order founded by Charles de Foucauld.

Some of the passages in Gandhi's story impressed me mightily. He would say that nonviolence is as old as the hills—that anyone could fight by nonviolent means and respect the dignity of the human person. They would ask Gandhi where he got his strength, and he would answer, "In the old holy books of India—and in the gospel, especially . . . in the Sermon on the Mount." So then his friends would ask him why he wasn't a Christian. And he would counter, "I shall be a Christian when I see the Christians living their Master's teaching." This was like a bolt from the blue for me. So there's a difference between talking and doing! We understand the gospel perfectly well, of course—intellectually, that is. But then we're supposed to go out and be consistent. That's the hard part.

So my progress was very gradual. I discovered Lanza del Vasto, too. He came to Argentina and started giving his talks on nonviolence. That was twenty-five or thirty years ago, I don't remember very well. I must have been about eighteen. I read some things by him too.

In Argentina there were youth movements, like the J.U.C.— the Catholic College Youth. They were very active, very much influenced by Pierre Teilhard de Chardin. But to tell the truth I really didn't have much contact with them. I had friends— nothing on an organized basis—and we would just get together to talk or study. I didn't belong to any organized church groups. Just informal groups. If we were asked to do something, we were glad to do it, but we weren't interested in anything too formal.

Meanwhile though, the writings of Teilhard were showing me another dimension of the church.

Coordinating Basic Movements

Then I got to know people already working in the nonviolent movement, like Hildegard Goss-Mayr and Jean Goss from Austria, who started out with Dom Hélder Câmara in Brazil when he was auxiliary bishop of Rio de Janeiro. They were the ones, by the way, who started to coordinate different activities, here and there and all over.

You see, there were groups working all over Argentina on a kind of liberation education in the spirit of nonviolence. There were a number of people working this way—Dom Hélder Câmara, Bishop Proaño in Ecuador, Cardinal Arns and Archbishop José Maria Pires in Brazil, Archbishop Jorge Manrique in Bolivia, and so on. But they weren't in very close contact with one another. They knew each other, and that was all one could say at that time. It was this need for communication and mutual support that furnished the impetus for our Peace and Justice Service. Alone we could do nothing. Together we could do a great deal.

Right from the start, the service was very careful not to be a movement. We thought things hadn't come together enough for that. We wanted something very modest, something that would grow as different needs came up. We started the service as a concrete way of supporting what was going on in dioceses, peasant groups, or workers' groups—all these groups that we put in contact with one another.

Meanwhile, we had to have a nonviolent strategy. It's true there were plenty of different activities all over—but all of them were separate actions, and they tended to peter out pretty quickly. There had to be channels for communication and support. For instance, along with Bishop Proaño in the fight the peasants were having to keep their land, we started up an international solidarity action—pressure on the governments as well as support for the bishop and mission groups.* I went to Ecuador several times to

*See below, Chapter 3, "Torment on the Plateau: The Indians' Story," pp. 71–91.

get that action going. Then a little later, when the peasants started having trouble in Paraguay at Garay and Jejuí, where a violent act of repression was committed, we helped Bishop Ramón Bogarín of San Juan Bautista de las Misiones and Auxiliary Bishop Aníbal Maricevich of Concepción to get a support action started there.*

So I wasn't working alone. It wasn't just one person doing it. Besides, the whole thing came out of the Medellín Conference in 1968. We followed that development with great interest. It was a pretty rough time for the church. The church was faced with enormous opportunities, but wasn't taking a clear stand anywhere—it wasn't taking any forthright options. It was still a do-good church. I think it was Medellín that gave us our motivation to go out to the poor—the motivation for a church that would be more poor, more prophetic, more committed to witness. Medellín had huge repercussions on all the movements.

Sharing Our Experiences

Our Peace and Justice Service grew by degrees. It all started in Montevideo with a little group of people. There was the Reverend Smith, a Methodist minister who ran a little newsletter. That was all there was. Then in 1971 we had another meeting—in Costa Rica in Central America—at Alajuela. There were Latin American groups, of course, but we also met European and North American groups that were working along our same lines.

In 1974 we went to the major seminary in Medellín, and our service acquired a bit more structure and organization. We had seventy-five delegates from twenty-two countries. That was where they asked me to become the secretary for the whole of Latin America. The theme of that meeting was the Strategy of Nonviolence in Latin America. There was a keynote address by Bishop Fragoso, and then Jean Goss spoke on evangelical nonviolence as a liberation force. There were other subjects, too, big ones. We even had non-Latins speaking, like Jean-Marie Muller. But the main thing was to find out what was going on in other countries. Nobody but the Latin Americans could vote. The

*See below, Chapter 4, "The Peasants' Battle for Survival," pp. 92–116.

others were observers; they took part in the debates, but didn't actually vote. For fifteen or twenty years the International Fellowship of Reconciliation had been working in certain Latin American countries. Now our service took this over—absorbed the actions of the fellowship.

In 1975 we met again—a meeting of Latin Americans this time in Buenos Aires at the motherhouse of the Institute Sisters at San Miguel. There were fifty or so of us from all the countries of Latin America. This time what we did was to exchange experiences and to conduct some training in nonviolent methods. And this is where we answered a call from comrades and priests in Paraguay when a repressive incident was going on at Jejuí. After the meeting I left for Paraguay to set up a whole campaign with Archbishop Silvero Rolón and Bishop Maricevich. It was a very hard time for the basic communities.

Then there were other meetings, but on a national basis—in Brazil, for instance.

In Argentina, we tried to get the people motivated about the problem of terrorism. It had been getting really vicious since about 1972. We tried pressuring the Congress, and we had some senators and bishops working with us on that action, but with no success. And so in 1975 some people began setting up what was to become the Permanent Assembly for Human Rights, composed of representatives from politics, the unions, and cooperatives. What this organization does today is to work on missing persons cases, the legal end of it. We were concerned about the lack of Christians in this effort. We had a loose coordination going on among Christian organizations, but it was barely creaking along. No success at all.

During the next year we started the Ecumenical Movement for Human Rights, modelling it on the Permanent Assembly. We wanted to have a movement of Christians like the one in Chile under the Solidarity Vicariate of the Archdiocese of Santiago. Today all these organizations are completely autonomous and have their own structures. As for the Peace and Justice Service, it was working with groups of the Mothers of the Plaza de Mayo.*

We have tried to stay in touch with the institutional church

*See below, Chapter 1, "The 'Mothers Courage' of Buenos Aires," pp. 43–57.

in all these activities as much as we can. Our Peace and Justice
Service has connections with the Argentine Bishops' Justice and
Peace Commission. But this kind of commission doesn't always
work out very well in Latin America. It may in Europe. In Argentina it can hardly do a thing. As for the Vatican Commission,
we're in constant contact.

As we kept holding all these meetings, we came to the conclusion that we had to give up any "charity," any social-work kind
of thing. It doesn't change things. It helps maintain the status
quo, and often simply bolsters the prevailing system. An emergency is different. But as an ongoing proposition, do-gooding is
no help at all. The important thing is to awaken a critical consciousness in the basic communities, so they can find their own
solutions to their problems. We try to offer very concrete support
to bishops, priests, missionaries, and the basic communities. We
work right with the grassroots—no milling about on the hilltops.
What we want to do is motivate the popular sectors.

We have a favorite idea, a kind of basic maxim: The first step
toward liberation, we say, occurs when a human being becomes
aware that he or she is a person. And our other favorite notion is
that the Christians of Latin America have a great deal to contribute to the process of the liberation of the peoples of the world.

More Terrible than an Armed Uprising:
The Peaceable Denunciation of Repression

We have never been without repression. Our problems are continuous.

And so it happened that in 1975 we went to Brazil to meet with
Cardinal Arns and set up a meeting of bishops in Colombia. It
was thought that it would be a good idea for some bishops who
knew one another, who were friends, to get together and reflect
on the evangelical power of nonviolence and to coordinate the
work going on in all their dioceses. But the moment we arrived,
we were arrested. Hoods were put over our heads, and we were
questioned all night long. I was with Hildegard Goss-Mayr and
Mario Carvalho de Jesús of the National Labor Front in São
Paulo. All three of us were arrested. Thanks to the cardinal's
intervention, we were released, but we were ordered out of Brazil.

Here is repression that is perfectly understandable. It's true we don't take up arms, but we have another type of action, a more troublesome one: the truth. We denounce injustice and try to raise people's consciousness. Then the people discover that they themselves have to find the answer to situations of injustice.

We started a campaign in Bolivia with the JOC (Young Catholic Workers) and the COB (Bolivian Labor Organization). We denounced the oppression that was hammering away at the Justice and Peace Commission of Bolivia. The commission had denounced a massacre in Cochabamba Valley in 1974. Wanting to see how we could help, we launched an international campaign on behalf of the jailed labor leaders and some religious who had been locked up as well. The religious were finally expelled from the country.

So the repression we were subjected to is not hard to understand. Personally I don't know how many times I've been arrested, say, for a day after a demonstration.

Everybody remembers the arrests at Riobamba in Ecuador in August 1976. We had gone there on the invitation of Bishop Proaño. Sixteen other bishops came too, and we shared our experiences, evaluated pastoral work, reflected on objectives to pursue, and tried to figure out ways of keeping in communication with one another—in other words, the sort of thing these bishops do from time to time anyway, the things Pope Paul VI had encouraged. The pope had said you ought to get together to exchange ideas, review your pastoral work—a mutual enrichment kind of thing. We were arrested right in the middle of the meeting, held for twenty-four hours, and then expelled from the country.

My last arrest in Argentina was for fourteen months, followed by fourteen more months under surveillance.

It started out with thirty-two days in what they call "the Pipe"—a very narrow, L-shaped cell just long enough for a prisoner to lie down in, with a little space at the door to stand up in. I was in the Pipe for thirty-two days.

"God Doesn't Kill"

Prison—well, I got through it in different ways. As far as I'm concerned, it's important to keep enough serenity inside you, by means of prayer, to hear God's silence, you might say—hear what God's trying to tell us in our personal life and in the signs of the times, and to see how we're living the signs of the times.

Certain things took on a special meaning for me. I was arrested on April 4—the Monday of Holy Week. It was the anniversary of the death of Martin Luther King, Jr., too. So I had quite a special Holy Week that year.

For the first two days in the Pipe it was completely dark. On the third day the guards opened the door, and the light came in. All of a sudden I could see dozens and dozens of graffiti—names of dear ones, prayers, insults, all sorts of things. Scribbled across some of the prayers was "In the evening of your life you'll be judged on your love," and "Holy Virgin, we're innocent," and "Father, forgive them for they know not what they do."

But what struck me most was a huge bloodstain, and an inscription below it scrawled by somebody's finger dipped in the blood: "God doesn't kill." Ever since, that inscription has remained engraved somewhere on my insides. It will be there all my life! These are the things that leave their mark on you—right while you're being tortured.

While I was in the Pipe, I wrote two letters and managed to have them transmitted to their addressees. I wrote them on tissue paper, one to Bishop Fragoso of Crateus in Brazil, and the other to friends of the movement in São Paulo. Here is the one to São Paulo:

April 20, 1977

Dear Mario, Alamiro, Carmen, Salvador, and everybody,

I won't write about suffering, I want to write about hope— about the grace Our Lord gives us to share with our brothers and sisters who are the victims of injustice—who after two years or longer in prison still don't know why they're being punished.

Yet there's always a light shining, to clarify and explain all these trials—God's presence every moment in every move—the God of love who forgives from the cross, down across the ages: "Father, forgive them; they do not know what they are doing."

Here in prison I've lived Holy Week in the grace of a greater understanding of the commitment, sacrifice, and love of Christ who shed his blood for everyone, for all humanity. What Easter gladness—the gladness of Christ as he triumphs by love, Christ risen and right here! Alleluia!

Bars can't lock up the Spirit—who is Christ's love dwelling with its infinite presence in every one of us.

Even those who doubt God receive his grace.

The cell walls are covered with prayers, with acts of faith and hope.

To live and share and walk with those who suffer! Blessed are they! We only ask to be faithful to his Word, and to live in his love.

Here everything is taken. We are naked before God, with our fears, our questions, our pain—but in all confidence in his grace.

That's where my hope is.

The Lord guide you, and give you his peace, his strength, and his joy.

Adolfo

P.S. I don't know what's going to happen. I'm waiting in trust. The work must go on: Christian witness, in spite of our limitations and weaknesses—united in prayer.

Missing Person

But to back up a bit—I was arrested at federal police headquarters. I had gone there to have my passport renewed. I had to have it in order to visit Bishop Proaño, since I was supposed to keep track of the work up there. But when I went into the downstairs office where you usually renew passports, they told me, "Go on upstairs, they'll give it to you up there."

When I got upstairs, two policemen were waiting for me. They took me into an office, and that's where I stayed. But I had had a friend with me, and he saw what happened and got out fast. He went straight to tell my wife. When she appeared on the scene, the police started to tell her they hadn't arrested me. But she said, "How can you say that? I was right here!"

If it hadn't been for my wife, I would just be one more missing person. In fact, the papers did report, for several days, "Pérez Esquivel missing." Evidently the police didn't want to admit I had been arrested. But then my wife came back with some attorneys and declared: "I was with my husband at police headquarters when he came to renew his passport. He was arrested here." Her firmness of mind was the determining factor.

I was on the fourth floor of the jail. There were not many people there. After a few days they let me walk around a bit. I was in a tiny room, but at least I could get the numbness out of my legs. I saw lots of women coming in groups. Some were released at three or four in the morning, without money, without papers, without anything. You have to remember, we were under martial law—you couldn't be going around at those hours of the morning. After a year or two in jail, these women would leave in terrible fear. Sometimes they were from the country, and didn't know Buenos Aires. I used to show them where they could go—to a religious house, to friends of mine, where the brothers would give them a bite to eat and a little money to get back home. After I got out of the Pipe, I could see where these women were being released. They had blindfolds there and all the things the guards used for the prisoners.

At this point in my imprisonment I hadn't been tortured yet.

When I was locked up in the Pipe, I could only leave to go to the toilet at set times. After a few days, though, they did let my wife bring something for me to eat on a daily basis. After a lot of insisting, Bishop Justo Laguna of San Isidro received authorization to see me. He was given three minutes in the presence of a guard. It was the first week in Lent. Beginning then, and all the time I was in jail, a priest would come to give me Communion once a week. My wife had managed to obtain this permission. Another priest came to see me several times too—Jorge Casarreto from San Isidro Diocese, who is now bishop of Rafaela. My wife, Amanda, came every week, except when I was "in punishment"—then you couldn't have visitors. I was too sore from the beatings anyway.

I never underwent any interrogation. I was never told why I had been arrested. Even today I don't know. They never gave me a reason.

Beaten and Tortured

Then what is the purpose of putting you away? Simply to destroy you. Psychologically and physically. I was in Unit Nine, in maximum security quarters. We were treated severely—constant body searches, with blows and all manner of annoyances. But the worst was to hear your comrades crying out when they were being beaten or moved to another jail. We would hear them getting out of the trucks. It would be about three or four in the morning, and we could hear the blows of the guards and the cries of the prisoners. It was awful.

Then I was tortured and thrown into the punishment cell, a real dungeon, a place they called the Sty. This was a terribly difficult time. But the worst thing, the most fearsome thing, was not the beatings they gave me or what they made me do—it was always the cries of my comrades. That was horrible, inhuman.

They tried to get me to insult God or the Blessed Virgin or bishops I knew. You couldn't have a Bible. That was forbidden, no matter how many times we asked. Father Casarreto tried to get me permission to have a book of the gospels. Nothing doing. When you asked them why, they always said, "Because it's forbidden." It was as simple as that. When I arrived there, I had a copy of Carlo Carretto's *Letters from the Desert* in my pocket. They took that. Any textbook or spiritual reading was forbidden. No exceptions. In fact, no manual activity was permitted at all.

What a strange thing it was to make people insult God for the defense of western Christian civilization! I never could make any sense of it. As far as I can see, that isn't what Christianity is about—using methods to crush and destroy a brother or a sister who is a child of God just as much as you are. It always struck me as farcical.

The one who passed out the insults was one of the higher-ups of the prison. He always had a couple of other officers with him. I don't know their names. They never identified themselves. The ones who administered the beatings were other officers and noncoms. This was normal treatment—very hard treatment, very heavy psychological pressure, attacks on your morale. Beatings. Cold showers at all hours of the night. We weren't given a towel, so I would jump up and down in my cell to try to get warm afterwards. Our garments were in tatters, and at night all you got was a straw mat and one blanket, even in winter. It still hurts where they broke two of my ribs. They hit us good and hard, and it really hurt.

It was prayer that was my mainstay in prison. Exercise was forbidden. They would get us up at 5:00 A.M. and we would have a few minutes to wash up. I would use that time for yoga, and this helped keep me in shape.

After thirty-two days in Buenos Aires I was transferred to La Plata. I never knew why they flew me there. That was almost never done for such a short trip. I was all by myself, strapped into a seat, and it would have been simpler just to drive me there. At La Plata there's only one prisoner to a cell. It's a high-risk detention facility. I was thrown into the Sty for five days.

I'd like to end this part of my story with a quotation from Martin Luther King, Jr. "It's not the repression by the bad people that hurts—it's the silence of the good."

The sin of omission—the refusal to get involved—is one of the worst things in the world. Christ calls us to get involved in the service of our sisters and brothers. It is in them, the bishops at Puebla tell us, that we must recognize his face. Martin Luther King's idea certainly applies here, because the evils in Latin America, as in so many other places, are the result of the silence of the good, the silence of those who don't get really and deeply involved with their brothers and sisters. I've thought a lot about this—the silence of the good. Involvement always costs. It's not hard to understand why we have been the victims of repression and persecution.

Pastors Close to the Poor

I mentioned earlier that while I was in jail some of the military people tried to get me to say something against bishops who were my friends.

Nonviolence generates close friendships. I have friends like

Bishop Fragoso, Bishop Proaño, and Cardinal Arns. I have paid them visits in their dioceses.

Bishop Fragoso comes to Argentina to see me every year. This year we even organized a meeting of three or four dozen basic communities. What impresses me about Bishop Fragoso is that he lives consistently. By that I mean there's no difference between what he says and what he does. The church of Crateus is a truly poor church, a prophetic one—a witnessing church. He stays involved, and proclaims a gospel that truly frees, a gospel that liberates all human beings. He proclaims the gospel in its spiritual dimension and in its social dimension. Bishop Fragoso has given land in his diocese to the peasants. He is always there among them when they most need him, when things are hardest. Every couple of weeks he writes me his suggestions, proposals, and directions for work in Latin America. This is no paternalistic bishop, surveying things from on high. This is a pastor who walks with his people.

The other bishop who has helped us a great deal is Bishop Proaño. And we have helped him a great deal as well—helped him in his work, helped him in his good times and bad, helped him in the attacks he has had to face. What has always struck me about him is his humility. You know about the Riobamba Cathedral. It collapsed, and only the great stone door sculpted by the Indians remained. And he left it like that. So the big landowners castigated him. He was not rebuilding the cathedral. And he said, "It will be rebuilt . . . but before we rebuild a cathedral of stone, we have to build one in the hearts of human beings." There I see a symbol—a sign of Bishop Proaño's involvement. He's in the midst of his people. I went with him to the mountains where he goes to celebrate the Eucharist with the Indian communities. He speaks with the peasants. The peasants recognize him as a real pastor, someone who lives the life of the people.

I went to São Paulo to see Cardinal Arns when the pope was in Brazil. I was in the stadium in Morumbi when John Paul II spoke to the workers. The pope sent a shock wave rolling through the masses of the people when he voiced support for the church's liberation effort. His support for Cardinal Arns, Dom Hélder Câmara, and Cardinal Aloisio Lorscheider was most significant. I believe the pope learned a great deal about Latin America as well. Just as in Mexico, he made changes in his prepared addresses as he went along. I think he understands our real situation here better than when he came to Puebla in Mexico. Here is a person who knows how to listen. It was a remarkable thing to see how in Brazil the pope listened to what the people had to say to him. This is important. This is an attitude not many pastors have. For instance, there was his reaction to the placards that said, "The people are hungry." Or the way he embraced Dallari, the lawyer who had escaped an assassination attempt, when Dallari got up to read the epistle at the papal Mass. So the Brazilian government's attitude is not hard to understand. There was no one from the government at the pope's departure ceremony. A most revealing attitude. For these self-styled Christian governments, there comes a moment of truth.

Is Nonviolence Effective?

"Nonviolence" is not a very good word for what we are trying to do. It makes you think of something negative. Many people think it means passivity. Our friends in Brazil, where the movement is more advanced, call it "maintained fidelity" or "steadfastness."* Martin Luther King, Jr., used to call it "the power of love." Gandhi didn't like "nonviolence" either—he preferred *satyagraha* or the "power of the truth." That is what we mean. If we say "nonviolence," it is only because we haven't found a better word. And after all, it is the word universally used for our struggle. So we keep using it.

Our work goes on at different levels. First—before any other steps in the liberation process—a human being must become aware that he or she is a person. Our approach is rooted in the gospel. We must transmit a Word of God that liberates, that frees human beings and their structures alike. Otherwise we are not preaching the gospel; we are preaching something else. We have to see how to get the gospel into all the areas of human life, all the areas of economics, politics, and culture. We have to see how to keep transforming this situation, how to keep moving toward hu-

---

*See below, Chapter 2, "The 150 Months of Resistance: The 'Snarlers' of the Perús Cement Company," pp. 58-70.

man liberation on both the spiritual and the social levels. For me the gospel isn't just personal. It needs to be shared.

We know too that one evil cannot be cured by another. Evils don't cancel each other out. They total up. Christ gives us a commandment, the commandment of love. He also gives us another commandment that is important for us: "You shall not kill." And that's it. That's plain. But we find all kinds of excuses. When human beings forget one another, they forget God—and thereby they give up their whole reason for existing. What good is culture, philosophy, or science if men and women become objects instead of subjects? We have always questioned armed liberation movements—for fear today's oppressed will become tomorrow's oppressors. If a human being is an object—just something to be used and thrown away—if every economic, political, or military project comes before persons—then what good are the things of this creation?

Where does nonviolence get its power?

First of all, from the active participation of its base—popular resistance. Next, from the application of methods of resisting aggression and injustice. These methods are worked out as a function of the opportunities that arise. There are no ready-made formulas. Formulas only come into being after situations are studied and analyzed. Our methodology is simple: from reflection to action and back to reflection again. We try to size up a situation of conflict, and carefully consider what is motivating the people involved in it. And there is another very important point: We try to act in truth. This is what gives our movement its security: the truth—respect for the human person. Respect for the human person generates constancy and steadfastness. And constancy and steadfastness generate an attack on evil and the possibility of altering the structures of injustice.

I'd like to call attention to a very important document: Archbishop José María Pires's pastoral letter to the peasants of Alagamar in Brazil's Northeast.* If someone is looking for a reference manual, this is it. Our method is based on practice, not on intellectual reflection.

*See below, "Pastoral Letter on the Church's Commitment to the Weak and Oppressed" by Archbishop José María Pires, pp. 93–101.

Isolation is an obstacle to the effectiveness of nonviolent action. So we try to coordinate what is being done almost everywhere. But the precise means vary considerably from country to country. In some places we have no secretariat, so we try to set up regional ones for in-depth work in all those countries together. Formerly, everything was concentrated in Buenos Aires and under our responsibility. We realized that we had to have secretariats in other countries like Chile or Brazil, and now we have people there in charge of the southern region. In Panama we have a secretariat for Central America and the Caribbean. In the Andean region we are just about to set up an office. We already have a good many contacts with people in that region, for example, in Ecuador, Colombia, Peru, and Bolivia.

Obviously, work in some countries will be more difficult than in others, where there is repression or lots of changes in personnel. This is the case in Paraguay and Uruguay. In Chile, on the other hand, the movement has made great strides. I went there recently and found an astonishing degree of mobilization all over the country. In early November 1980, we had a meeting of the whole southern region in Santiago at which there were talks by bishops like Bishop Jorge Hourton and Bishop Enrique Alvear. Then I was able to work with some groups—political parties, actually—including the Group of Twenty-Four, which is made up of people of various political views. Next there were pastoral projects with workers or students at universities, where I have given some talks. Then, there are contacts with churches—with the Catholic church and especially with Cardinal Raúl Silva—the Solidarity Vicariate, and the Ecumenical Fraternity, where a permanent Committee for Peace has been set up. So we had a week of rather intense activity—even if the Chilean authorities did refuse to see us.

Some say there's nothing to be achieved by these methods. But we actually see their positive results. When Dom Hélder Câmara began to work this way years ago, he was just a voice in the wilderness, and now the movement has spread all over Latin America.

The church is taking on a new face, a new dimension—the dimension of involvement. I believe that the church has taken the step from being a church-for-the-people to being a church-with-the-people. In Brazil it has grown to be a real force. The more conservative elements keep losing ground. Of course, there are inconsistencies, but there's forward motion, too, and now there's no turning back.

When we say "church," we shouldn't just think of the hierarchy, but of the church's base as well. The Christian people have made their commitment, and it is they who are insisting on a more complete conversion. As far as I'm concerned, the biggest changes don't happen from the top down, they happen from the bottom up. It's the power in the base that is going to transform the structures.

There are divisions in the church; this is true. Some bishops need conversion. They need to discover the involvement dimension. It is always painful to see some bishops living practically like princes when Our Lord became poor and wanted to be the least of all people. But to me it's a very important event, full of promise, to have the church taking a different way now and becoming poor and prophetic—an Easter church. A certain number of involved bishops are opening up this new vision of the church. They're going back to the gospel approach of evangelizing the poor— preaching the gospel to the poor, to the masses of the people. Yesterday the church looked at the world from the outside. Today the church has entered the world to evangelize it from the inside and lead it to God. It is this movement in the church that has awakened a new awareness within the people—a new spiritual life.

Is Armed Resistance Justified in the Current Situation?

As we consider the question of the effectiveness of non-violence, we have Nicaragua staring us in the face. "The Sandinist Revolution has triumphed." Doesn't this demonstrate the justifiability of violence for liberation?

I think the historical circumstances of the Nicaraguan Revolution have to be looked at more closely. When the masses of the people have their backs to the wall of despair—when they see no other alternative—they seem to *have* to have recourse to violence. Their attitude is justifiable. Only I don't agree with the method. When you're desperate, you have recourse to anything you can lay your hands on. But that doesn't make it right, and it doesn't make it effective. Some say you have to fight fire with fire. The only trouble with that argument is that fire is still fire. Recently I sat at a round table in Geneva with people from African countries. One of them said something that especially struck me. "For centuries," he said, "we lived under white domination. Now we live under black domination. This is progress?"

I don't think the Nicaraguan Revolution was just the result of military action. We have to look at the problem in its totality, not just partially. For a number of years the Sandinist forces had harrassed the government of President Anastasio Somoza, but couldn't shake it. They were like a mosquito bite—a nuisance, and that's all! The Sandinists were nearly wiped out. Then certain things happened. And a nonviolent struggle on the part of the people was unleashed—an intense, extremely important struggle to which we have not paid enough attention.

In the Nicaraguan Revolution there was a truly popular uprising from the moment the dominators assassinated journalist Pedro Chamorro in January 1978. It was the precise, concrete fact of Chamorro's murder that provoked the popular indignation against Somoza's dictatorship—on all levels—and it was an indignation that resulted in an uprising of the people, a popular insurrection. That was a nonviolent struggle. What the *people* were doing was nonviolent. The Sandinists only took advantage of that situation to regain their credibility in the eyes of the people, a credibility they had not enjoyed for years. An armed revolt cannot succeed without an insurgency, an uprising of the collective consciousness.

But now let us look deeper still. There was another factor: Somoza's international isolation, especially from the United States, an isolation that became definitive the day an American journalist was murdered in Nicaragua in front of television cameras in June 1979. If we look at the newspapers of about that time, we see that Somoza made a trip to the United States to beg for American economic and military support—and that when he got back, he declared that his great friend to the north had abandoned him. His isolation was something very real then, and it was due to the reaction of the American people themselves. From that moment on, the Somoza regime was practically bound to fall. And now the Sandinists come back onto the stage. Faced by the choice of giving support to Somoza or giving support to the Sandinists, the people of Nicaragua logically opted for the Sandinists. And then Somoza's collapse was complete.

So when people talk about a Sandinist guerrilla revolution, they're taking a very partial view of things. As far as I can see, it was the Nicaraguan people who conducted the revolution and not just the Sandinists. And today we hear of reactions within the government that confirm what I've been saying: We're afraid that today's oppressed may become tomorrow's oppressors. That is what the African in Geneva was saying about his own people.

Liberation from Armed Constraint

The theology of liberation is very important and has made a fine contribution to the Latin American church. But I think it needs deepening and development. It is not yet a complete theology. It needs continued involvement in order to be able to furnish answers to the questions of our times.

We might put it this way: This theology has not yet made sufficient room for a reflection on nonviolence. Some theologians seem to verge on taking this step, but by and large the theology of liberation has not yet discovered that nonviolence is a force capable of truly liberating without becoming an armed might. The theology of liberation has as yet given us no clear answer to the question of the actual means of liberation. But then neither has the church as a whole.

Many reject violence, but see no other course—no other alternative, no other option to follow. For us there is an alternative: nonviolence. Nonviolence is a challenge, but it is the only option for us as Christians if we wish to effect changes in depth. This is what we were beginning to reflect upon at a meeting on nonviolence we held in Bogotá.*

You see, it's not just a method of fighting. It's not just a mechanism, so that all you'd have to do is to put it in gear. It's a manner of being, a way of living. I think we're breaking new ground. Certain of the bishops are very deeply impressed by the non-

*See below, Appendix A, "Latin America's Charter of Nonviolence," pp. 117–135.

violent approach, and use it as an active praxis. But we need many more meetings and much more reflection—and, above all, much more experience in the field. We're taking baby steps. We're looking at what the theology of liberation could contribute to nonviolence. For that matter we generally keep our ear to the ground: We're not an organization that suffers from an overload of structures or means. And then too I often say: We don't have all that much to talk about; we have a lot to share.

Refusing to Play by the Rules

I have a couple of very simple ways of explaining the nonviolent method.[1] When you play chess or checkers, you and your opponent have to agree to play by the same rules; otherwise the game simply can't take place. Well, in nonviolent combat what we do is just exactly what nice players aren't supposed to do. We refuse to play by one of the rules the system tries to foist on us: the rule that says you have to counter violence with violence. If your opponents can get you to swallow that idea, then they can unleash still greater violence on you. The essential thing in nonviolent combat is for us to render these tactics inoperative by refusing to play by the rules and by imposing our own conditions instead.

The other example—a very simple one that makes people smile—is that of the battle of the ant and the elephant. True, the elephant is stronger. But the ants . . . well, there are more of us. That's why the basic communities are so important; that's why we absolutely have to have basic groups. The basic community has some unique characteristics: It enables each member to find himself or herself as a person. It develops a sense of solidarity, a sense of a community of brothers and sisters. That is precisely what the bishops at Puebla were talking about when they called for communion and participation. Here is a mighty force for changing the structures of injustice that mark our society.

Our great hope and encouragement, as we keep organizing the people, is knowing we're getting somewhere. When we look at the people of Latin America today, we see that they have acquired a critical consciousness. They are not the same as they were fifteen or twenty years ago. They understand their situation much better. And they demand a concrete response to their problems. Violence is certainly on the increase everywhere, especially in Central America. But what does that mean? It means there's very, very strong pressure from the base, and that this pressure is provoking a repressive reaction.

There are those who accuse us of playing into the hands of communism by criticizing the prevailing system. We reject this accusation. We are no more playing inth the hands of communism by criticizing the system than we are playing into the hands of rightist systems. Terrorism by definition consists of terror. Terrorism of the left and terrorism of the right only add up. They never offer a solution to problems. To me, terrorism, no matter what its source, is an attack on the human being, on humanity, on God. Hence we reject terrorism in all its forms. It leads nowhere because nothing can be built on it. Leftist extremist groups say they're using terror for the liberation of the people. But with terror you liberate nothing. State terrorists say they're practicing terrorism because their backs are to the wall—they've been forced into this "dirty war," and they're only using the same methods to defend what they call "western Christian civilization." But they're not defending a thing! They're defending themselves and their shabby little interests, that's all. They're not defending the dignity of the human person. They're not defending the people.

Sometimes the basic communities take up arms. This is what is happening in El Salvador. It's understandable for a community to become political. Politics is necessary. It's with political alternatives to the system that you straighten out society's problems. Goodwill isn't enough. But if the communities go radical and choose to take up arms, it's because they feel driven into a corner and no longer see any other way out. No one has offered them an alternative. The alternative is a popular uprising, like the one that took place in Nicaragua.

Which Society Do We Choose?

Some people tell us our only choice is between capitalism and communism, and that the revolution is therefore going to have to take us one way or the other.

Personally, I would prefer it take us neither way. We must find an alternative. The alternative will be a form of socialization. I fail to see why this necessarily has to be communism. Capitalism and communism are both imperialisms that provide only half answers. They make the human being an object. So to my way of thinking Christians in Latin America have a particular responsibility to find political alternatives.

At the moment there is no such thing as a noncommunist socialism. It has to be invented. We have no ready-made formulas and no pat answers. In Brazil, for instance, the communities are actually working on political proposals. Our movement for nonviolence is studying political projects too. We want something besides capitalism or communism, something on the order of self-management and sharing. In fact, participation is the basic element we seek.

The Arms Race

In the conflict between Argentina and Chile, there is a very serious problem in the sale of arms by the industrialized nations. Thus, for example, France sells arms to both countries, reaping a profit from the potential that exists for armed conflict between Chile and Argentina. In Europe they keep saying that if you stop making weapons, you'll have to close the factories and there will be more unemployment. But could not this war economy be transformed into an economy for development and peace among the peoples? A Mirage costs more than $10 million, while misery stares us in the face. Children starve to death, families live in squalor, education and medical care are nonexistent. Think of what we could do with the price of a single Mirage! No one has the right to create an economy at the expense of the world's poor.

In considering the creative potential God has given us, I often wonder what the engineers, technicians, and workers who make weapons all day long for killing their neighbor can possibly be thinking of. They're not working for a living; they're working for dying. They're using their mental powers to manufacture weapons to kill one another better. I believe the church has a very heavy responsibility here to pressure consciences so that each person can reconsider his or her position.

Today it's no longer a question of nonviolence or violence. As

Martin Luther King, Jr., said, it's a question of nonviolence or nonexistence. If we stay on the road we're on, concerned only with the here-and-now and how to justify ourselves, what will be left for humanity? What kind of world are we building for our children and grandchildren? What do we think we are going to bequeath them, with all our nuclear arsenals, the burgeoning arms market, and a consumer society that swamps human persons and makes them slaves of the system?

This is certainly a problem of consumerism. We consume arms, we consume useless products, we consume everything in sight. And we end up by consuming human beings themselves.

There is an important task of education facing us, especially with our youth, lest they too be dragged into the consumer society we have created for ourselves. We must help them find life values, life's essential values. They must learn that a more just and humane world is possible only if we make ourselves our sisters' and brothers' servants—only if we live with our sisters and brothers in understanding, in sharing, and in communion. Otherwise we have accepted the despair that is invading our planet.

As for us in Latin America, we live on hope. We stand ready to fight until this world becomes a reality.

I had not made a trip back to Europe since 1976, when I didn't feel much sensitivity there for our Latin American problems. Today I'm struck to see how very concerned Europeans are about our problems. The European nations have grown in their critical awareness, in their sense of responsibility for the poor nations. I believe this is something very important and very positive. As for our making the problems of other peoples our own—this is a path we hope will open up ahead of us.

In the Name of Those Who Struggle in Latin America

When I was awarded the Nobel Prize for Peace, it was understood very well that I was receiving it in the name of the struggling people. My government pretended not to understand, but they understood—only too well.

The Nobel Prize was for our work in Latin America, our Christian involvement, our option for the poor. It is not my personal award. I received it in the name of all the peoples of Latin America, in the name of all who have no right to speak, in the name of all who are toiling in the same cause—peasants, working people, Indians, bishops, all who are together in the same task. I am but a part of the whole, and the lot fell on me. It could have been someone else.

The government reacted poorly, very poorly. It took them thirty-six hours to get up the following statement:

> The activity engaged in by . . . Pérez Esquivel . . . was, against his own intention, put to use by others to secure the impunity of members of various terrorist groups.

We have to say that this is rather a subjective view of things. The statement speaks of terrorism. Terrorism of the left, of course. What about state terrorism?

There were some ambiguous reactions on the part of bishops, too. They have their view, and I respect that view, but we're going ahead now in the direction of the commitment we've made. In some cases any divergencies we may have are minimal. The friendship that binds us is stronger.

With the Nobel Prize I especially don't forget the Indians, in particular, the ones in Ecuador who always have a place for me when I go there.

On one of my first trips to Ecuador, I had a dream. I dreamt I saw Christ on the cross dressed in a poncho. Later I went to Riobamba, and happened to be visiting a community of the Little Brothers of Jesus founded by Charles de Foucauld. I went into the chapel and there he was on the wall again—Christ crucified, in a poncho, as I had seen him in my dream. The image wasn't exactly the same, but it was Christ in a poncho. This struck me very much, and from then on he never let me alone.

As an artist I have practically no time right now to do any work at all. But after I was released from La Plata Prison, I set myself to do a painting of *Christ in a Poncho*.

He is the Christ of the poor. And he is a Christ without a face or hands or feet, for his face, hands, and feet are the faces, hands, and feet of the Indians and peasants of Latin America. Christ in a poncho is the presence of Christ in the poor, this continuous presence of which Puebla speaks so well—so much so that when I read the Final Document of the Puebla Conference, and came to the passage that speaks of the "very concrete faces" in which "we ought to recognize the suffering features of Christ the Lord, who questions and challenges us,"[2] I identified it with this vision that has so haunted me through the years.

PART TWO

Testimonials of Nonviolence

Conceived in southern Africa and born in India, nonviolence is the child of the insight and action of a particular person: Gandhi, the walking archetype of nonviolence.

In the United States Martin Luther King, Jr. left the mark of his personality on the strenuous fight of the American blacks. Although the blacks failed to carry the day they still made remarkable gains against all odds.

Here we have figures of international renown. Here we have giants of history.

Adolfo Pérez Esquivel and his nonviolent combat are different. The Latin American coordinator of the Peace and Justice Service is no mighty figure. He is more like an ant. For like an ant he works to open up new paths—to set up lines of communication among various groups at work all over Latin America. His labor is in the image of that of Sean McBride, the 1974 Nobel Peace Laureate. In creating Amnesty International, McBride only crystallized latent energies as he built up an ever broader network of relationships of solidarity. Pérez Esquivel can likewise take effective action. His support for the mothers of the Plaza de Mayo of Argentina stands as an example. Here he reminds us of Betty Williams and Mairead Corrigan, the Irish mothers who won the Nobel Prize in 1976. In the nonviolent movement Pérez Esquivel is a catalyst without whom the flourishing variety of individual nonviolent projects could never have crystallized into a movement.

The sudden projection of Pérez onto the front pages is a recognition of the value of the work of an ant. The great ones of this world stride solemnly to their conference tables, seat themselves, and attempt to surmount their difficult problems. The giants of economics fly by jet from a trilateral summit to their next multinational parley. Meanwhile, the lowly ant scrambles from hill to hill, thinking, "It is high time the little people, too, got organized."

Here is where we will do well to observe the remarkable experiment of Amnesty International. For the first time in the history of industrial societies a movement of public opinion has appeared whose end and aim are extrinsic to all corporate industrial enterprise. Today it is possible to mobilize the scattered energies of individuals in efficacious opposition to the arbitrary exercise of political power. Today for the first time in history we have a remedy for a basic injustice that places society's very survival in jeopardy.

One of the keenest frustrations of modern industrial civilization arises from the extreme disproportion between catastrophic information and effective remedy. There has been an epic development of the information media, thanks to the technological explosion of recent years. As a result, we have today the capacity to know at every moment everything that is occurring everywhere on our planet. But at the same time we are altogether incapable of action to modify the hideous happenings that assault our consciousness and our conscience. What can the average European or United States citizen do to put a stop to the machinations of a bloody tyrant, or the misdeeds of a multinational milk-products corporation that feeds on starving Third World babies, or the barbarity of a regime of terror?

Members of Amnesty International have learned by experience that, in the area of the defense of those imprisoned for their opinions, maximal information can produce an acceptable minimum of action and efficaciousness. All one need do is define one's object very closely and simply—then organize. Amnesty International has grown to be a group enterprise, a kind of spiritual energy conglomerate whose power has no further need of demonstration. What almighty chief of state today can convincingly boast indifference to a world pressure movement like this one?

Analogously, nonviolence in Latin America can become the locus and means of an organized popular movement. In today's industrial societies, the reality of the people has faded into the phenomenon of the anonymous crowd. We live in the kingdom of the indefinite pronoun, the era of the atomization and homogenization of individuals. But in countries still strongly marked by a rural cultural mentality (even in the sprawling suburbs of Latin America, where the people have come from the country), the sense of human community remains very much alive. The Amerindian communal or communitarian experience in Latin America is an ancestral heritage that has managed to survive to our own times. This gives much greater possibilities for organization to our region than to the countries of the Northern Hemisphere.

This has been well understood by a number of church people and Latin American Christians for some fifteen years. The key word in Latin American nonviolence is "organization."

And so arises the possibility of the type of actions Pérez Esquivel reports to us in the following pages. These documents exemplify the results of his work: the courageous, admirable obstinacy of Argentina's Plaza de Mayo Mothers; the firmness and perseverance of the Brazilian cement workers in São Paulo who won their cause after twelve years of battle; the struggle of the peasants or Indians in Ecuador, Brazil, or Paraguay to hold onto their lands.

Out of the kaleidoscopic situation of injustice and violence in Latin America there emerge certain testimonials that are particularly salient. These are hard, tragic experiences. But they are charged with hope.

1.

The "Mothers Courage" of Buenos Aires

During the weeks following General Videla's coup in March 1976, an ever greater number of mothers in distress went in search of the little Peace and Justice team of Buenos Aires. They were mourning the disappearance of a son or a daughter kidnapped by the security forces. The crisis of Argentina's missing persons had begun.

With the support of the Peace and Justice Service, the mothers at first simply encouraged one another to overcome their despair. One day it was suggested to them that they have a silent demonstration—in the Plaza de Mayo, the square right in the center of Buenos Aires and opposite the federal complex—until they should receive a response from the authorities. Ever since, the weekly marches of the Plaza de Mayo Mothers have been uninterrupted except by dispersal or arrest. But the authorities' response is very, very long in coming.

In reply to reporters' "innocent" questions concerning these strange processions, policemen would mutter something about "madwomen." And so the Mothers acquired a second sobriquet: the "Madwomen of the Plaza de Mayo."

Madwomen indeed. With the madness of ants attacking the elephant of brute force. With the obduracy of a mother's love, in a desperate appeal to whatever human sensitivity might still be in the heart of a despot. With the courage of defenseless women—some are "missing" now themselves—silently holding up a name *or a photograph before the downtown crowd: "Where is my child?"*

These are Pérez Esquivel's "Mothers Courage," face to face with the blind, dumb violence of state policy.

THE MOTHERS OF THE PLAZA DE MAYO

Document drawn up by a group of the Mothers of the Plaza de Mayo at the close of a meeting organized in July 1980, with the collaboration of the Peace and Justice Service, on "Gospel and the Experience of Human Community."

Nothing can do more human harm than the pain of such long years of uncertainty—of simply not knowing. The passing days, with their alternations of feeble, fading hope and hopeless depression, cause a grave deterioration of spirit and body. Fear like this deals heavy blows to the family unit it infests, progressively debilitating it until it is destroyed.

Grandparents have to rear their grandchildren themselves without the faintest notion of what the future may hold. They no longer have their sons and daughters at home. They must make all decisions alone.

Children's whole lives become a question mark. They do not know what has become of their parents. They do not know that their parents have been kidnapped, and that this is why they are no longer at home. The children only wonder "why they have gone away."

Brothers and sisters are so fearful for themselves and their families that they fail to cope with the vacuum left by their siblings' disappearance. They fear even to continue the search, for now they have to be concerned for their own safety and that of others.

Husbands and wives know nothing of their life companions.

How perniciously this cancer eats away at society. For we mothers are members of a society, and the tragedy that engulfs us must overflow until it pollutes the whole body politic. As mothers, then—for it is we mothers who must carry the daily burden of the family mood, with its joys and its travails—we have united among ourselves to share one another's burden in the hope of somehow being able to hold up under the concerns that weigh upon us so heavily. In spite of all—and above all—we desire to be able to vanquish this torment with our faith and hope and with the might of our very sorrow, and thereby somehow manage to continue, somehow manage to do something to find our children.

With all our hearts we wish and desire to help others. For in this way we shall help ourselves. We wish to be the goad that—somewhere and somehow—will be the occasion of something positive happening. We wish only to make some contribution toward doing away once and for all with this incredibly macabre hell where, in the very midst of modern civilization, the human mind is molded for human destruction.

We have found clear-headed, perceptive persons who can help us. After speaking with them, we now understand things better. In our search for the right path to take, and with the help of these same persons, we shall now endeavor to generate the "antibody" we need to build our strength for the struggle. The way will be long, but not fruitless. We have been asking ourselves questions. We have been analyzing our predicament and learning to listen. We have been acquiring a grasp of our political and economic situation. And above all, we have been fortifying and confirming our faith in God through spiritual exercises for the uplifting of mind and spirit.

Our meeting has borne much fruit. It has enabled us to come to an awareness of our rights and duties, and has afforded us the faith to exercise and discharge these rights and duties. It has strengthened our ability to understand and to share our understanding. What a responsibility! Women who had known only how to love their dear ones now suddenly know why these dear ones are suffering, and how they themselves must accompany them on the road of suffering!

Our need was sore, and we have met it. We have been considering the topic "Gospel and the Experience of Human Community."

And now we look to tomorrow. We know that much remains to be done. But we have begun to hope again. Now we have an expectation to which we can cling until such time as the storm is weathered and we have achieved a definitive, satisfactory solution. For tomorrow is what we make it, and it will be ours.

The Mothers of the Plaza de Mayo

THE TASK OF THE PEACE
AND JUSTICE SERVICE IN LATIN AMERICA

Statement by Adolfo Pérez Esquivel to the meeting on "Gospel and the Experience of Human Community" held by the Mothers of the Plaza de Mayo in July 1980.

The Peace and Justice Service in Latin America—a Christian organization—is, as its name indicates, a service. The service it attempts to render is the promotion of solidarity among the basic groups, movements, and Christian organizations involved in the integral liberation of human beings and peoples within an approach springing from Christian faith.

Christians are genuinely interested and involved in the problem-ridden reality of this rapidly changing life of human beings and society. The service comes forward to take its stand on behalf of the masses of the oppressed. It is a stand based on the profound meaning of the gospel, and it is the gospel that tells why we seek to share the people's journey.

To this end the service had chosen nonviolence as a gospel force for liberation in solidarity with the poorest and neediest of Latin America.

The service promotes alternatives for the building of a more just and humane society, taking human beings as it finds them, and moving out with them toward an action of spiritual and social transformation.

We seek to awaken a critical awareness in persons, so that they may recognize themselves as persons indeed, and thus be able to proceed to search out concrete paths toward an in-depth transformation of situations of injustice.

The service is born of an uneasiness and concern on the part of bishops, priests, religious, pastors, workers, peasants, and business and professional people. These individuals have all seen and experienced things in their countries that motivate them to undertake an effort of convergence, beginning with solidarity among themselves and then in turn with the people of Latin America.

The service maintains close ties of common effort and communion with similar organizations throughout the world—in Europe, the United States, Canada, and Asia—in projects of active involvement via its national and regional secretariats in Latin America.

Relations are likewise maintained with organizations like the International Fellowship of Reconciliation, Pax Christi International, Alternative Nonviolence, Justice and Peace Commissions, Peace People, and a variety of other nonviolent movements, as well as with the churches. And the list could go on.

Root of All Violence

Today problems affecting a people are no longer isolated phenomena; they have international repercussions. The communications media and news services bring concerns and situations together, laying them side-by-side before the eyes of a startled world in a great collage of problems—the ever more complex problems of the life of peoples in all parts of Latin America.

Thus today the situation in Argentina is added to the total of what is occurring or has occurred in other countries of Latin America. And thus it, too, is having its international repercussions. Our meeting has already examined the situation in Argentina. Now we must endeavor to grasp this situation in its total context of Latin American life.

It is no coincidence that most of our countries today live under military regimes and national security systems. This is what concerned the bishops gathered at Puebla de Los Angeles in Mexico to make an analysis of Latin American conditions. The rash of conflicts and violence assaulting the people is not just circumstantial or accidental. We must look for its root cause.

We find we do not have far to look. These situations of conflict and violence are the product of the prevailing economic, social, and political system.

We are in the presence of structural, institutionalized violence.

We are reaping the fruits of a system which, as Pope John Paul II puts it, makes the rich richer by making the poor poorer. In other words, injustice is the root of all other forms of violence—the root of all the misery, marginalization, and exploitation under which the majority of the Latin American people have to live because the great resources and wealth of our nations are concentrated in the hands of a privileged few.

The most basic necessities of health, education, housing, and distribution of wealth are missing for vast masses of the peasants and working people of Latin America.

We view it with concern when Christians or other persons of goodwill who, out of a sensitivity to human values, make a commitment to the transformation of situations of injustice, are automatically labeled "communists" and "subversives," and then persecuted for these labels. Those elements within the churches which, in their evangelical mission, take on an involvement with the poorest and neediest, are having to pay dearly for their concern by the repression they have to suffer at the hands of privileged minorities. Thus we already have a long list of peasants, young people, workers, priests, religious, and bishops—martyrs in our own time—who have suffered for merely seeking to build a more just and humane society.

Missing Persons

We in Argentina are confronted with the traumatic and inhuman situation of the missing persons—children who have disappeared, children born in prison and subsequently vanishing as well, persons jailed without due process and subjected to all manner of ill treatment.

And then we have to listen to the "defense of western Christian civilization" alleged as a justification for the peculiar methods used in what the oppressors themselves call this "dirty war"—by which they mean a war waged not only against actual guerrillas but also against all sectors of national life—business and professional people, students, religious, and popular organizations.

The voice of the people is mute, stifled by an authoritarian system that refuses to permit the solution of these problems. The regime does not even respond to the demands of international organizations like the Latin American Commission on Human Rights of the Organization of American States.

On other levels as well—the United Nations, church organizations, groups of jurists, democratic governments the world over—the prompt correction of these grave human rights violations has been demanded. But to no avail—no solution is in sight. We see only too clearly that the road will be a hard one. All demands—just demands for the restoration of civil rights, the return of missing persons, the implementation of the principles of due process and fair trial, and the release of prisoners held without trial or indictment—meet with a blank wall of complete insensitivity.

These demands have all been made hundreds of times. But there is no response.

Participation and Democracy

We simply have to find alternatives. We must find solutions to circumstantial and structural problems alike, for it is clear that questions concerning the violation of human rights are partly linked to society's global problems. What can we do, then, to uncover avenues to a solution? Where is our point of departure?

Among the conclusions you reached yesterday was a consensus on the role the Plaza de Mayo Mothers should play.

Your reflection in the course of this meeting has led you from the purely spontaneous and emotional actions you might undertake to an awareness that there are political and social problems to be faced. Many of you have taken the decision to embark on this course only reluctantly. But as the Mothers of the Plaza de Mayo, you have come to the conclusion that you must also take up your role as citizens. You must participate in politics and make your voices heard without taking sides with any particular party. And there is more: This new participation of yours implies that you will know how to face and handle your own problems yourselves. It implies a degree of maturity that will permit you to outline an action for yourselves and alternatives to strive for in view of specific pressures brought to bear by the prevailing system.

Our analysis of the current situation has demonstrated that the violations of human rights which we see around us are the product of a collision of two opposing models of society. One model is seeking to establish itself while the other is seeking to maintain itself in power. These models correspond to the respective interests of two opposing sectors of society. We have also seen how any efforts to achieve a greater popular participation in the political process, however limited, with a view to bringing about a more just and equitable society are restricted, impeded, and repressed. This is because such efforts contravene the dominant interests.

What we have seen in our work in this meeting enables us to sketch some alternatives to develop in the area of human rights—paths to follow in opposing the power of the dominators. In working out these alternatives and following these paths we shall be making a solid contribution to the development of the dynamics of participation so urgently demanded by our people.

Going Beyond Domination

You have been handed copies of documents prepared by the Brazilian Bishops' Conference and a number of other Christian organizations concerning their Project for a Society Beyond Domination. We have seen how these documents pose the challenge of beginning a historical process that will take us above and beyond the prevailing forms of domination. In this way we can collaborate in the construction of a more just community of sisters and brothers, a society of communion and regard for human rights. We shall then not permit the establishment of a new domination in place of the old one.

This, then, is one of the key questions: participation. In sociological terms it is called the "socialization of power and wealth." But the problem is how to achieve this participation now, and not in some distant future. How can we succeed in this aim?

The problem is a very complex one, for it concerns the whole world. In capitalist systems, popular participation and democracy are either reduced (in nations at the center of the capitalist world) or suspended (in nations at the periphery of this world) in the name of what is termed "economic development." This is one of the aspects of participation and democracy that the Trilateral

Commission[1] is attempting to regulate. According to the commission, such participation raises "too many" questions about the status quo and is hostile to the concentration of capital. Although the commission is favorable to efforts at democratization in Latin America, it prefers to see solutions in this area limited to the forms of democracy. For the commission is aware that it will not do to try to close the door to participation altogether.

Of course, participation and democracy also leave something to be desired in the leftist camp. They are "under discussion," we are told. The "socialist" nations, it would seem, have not yet succeeded in socializing political power. Thus they have fallen victim to a new form of domination. And domination is still domination, however different it may be from that prevailing in capitalist lands.

Our own work is much too humble and modest to attempt to resolve all these problems. But it can try to stimulate concrete experiments in participation—alternatives to domination consisting in the use of power for service—by means of which people can move out from wherever they may happen to find themselves in order to create a social ambience incompatible with our society's various forms of domination—an ambience that will sow the seeds of a culture of nondomination. This will require a process of our own reeducation, first and foremost. And from the very beginning it will require a project to mold a current of public opinion. In the long run this approach will benefit our whole people, and ensure a process of integral liberation that will be genuinely this people's own achievement. Their self-liberation must be the product of structures of participation in production and politics alike.

The documents distributed for discussion are to be seen as depicting the target, the utopia we are to strive for. Our means will consist in an ongoing, persevering process that we may begin today. The task lying before us is, first, to raise the people's consciousness with regard to human rights. And here our reflection and praxis will not be limited to a denunciation of the disregard of those rights. They will also comprise a presentation of the alternatives we envisage, alternatives that "go beyond domination," in the spirit of the bishops' documents. For the construction of a society in which human rights are accorded their due respect, the means most immediately available to us will consist in an enterprise of public education.

The Poor People's Weapon

Very well, but how shall we begin the fight?

Pope John Paul II shows us very clearly. He even provides us with a slogan: "The truth is a mighty force for peace." Only the truth will make us free (cf. John 8:32). It alone will empower us to find a solution to the difficult situation in which we live, so that we may at last have justice and peace. We know very well that peace is the fruit of justice, and that reconciliation can only be born of truth and justice.

How can we reflect upon and live our faith as we engage in this struggle? For we have chosen to struggle in the challenge of the Word. We have opted for a struggle that will be coherent with the gospel.

We struggle by rendering operative the force of love in the battle for liberation. Active nonviolence is a response, a step forward (whether the world realizes it or not) that is based on the gospel. We also find nonviolence in other religions besides Christianity.

Nonviolence is a way of answering evil and injustice with truth and hate with love. For truth and love are the weapons of the spirit in the face of repression.

Nonviolence is not passivity or conformism. It is a spirit, and a method. It is a spirit of prophecy, for it denounces all sundering of a community of brothers and sisters and proclaims that this community can only be rebuilt through love. And it is a method— an organized set of ruptures in the civil order so as to disturb the system responsible for the injustices we see around us.

Puebla itself sounded the call:

> Our responsibility as Christians is to use all possible means to promote the implementation of nonviolent tactics in the effort to re-establish justice in economic and political relations [no. 533].

The means are manifold, depending on the creative capabilities of the people. Here we see the power of the dispossessed, the weapon of the poor. The struggle, then, will be the people's struggle. Here is participation indeed. Here is no elitist contest, no partisan struggle of *foquistas*.[2] The means will include boycotts, strikes, noncooperation, civil disobedience, hunger strikes, and many other actions.

In virtue of its nature as a form of social and moral pressure, the liberating activity of nonviolence does not provoke a mobilization of the forces of the opposition. Nonviolence chooses too unfamiliar a field of combat. The opposition is accustomed to relying on fear and repressive force. Nonviolence proceeds by overcoming fear and by refusing to engage the enemy on terrain advantageous to them. As a result, the opponents are obliged to employ a different and unfamiliar means of defense—one having a higher political price tag. For now the system is not responding to the use of violence, which would have lent a tinge of legitimacy to the use of counterviolence. Instead, the system is responding to a peaceful struggle that can generally count on greater popular support and solidarity. As we move ahead with our action, we discover that this option is more democratic. It respects its popular base; it mobilizes the creativity of little people; and above all, it is more effective because it brings more people into the historical process of liberation.

As mothers, you know the power of love. You have been practicing it in your marches on the Plaza de Mayo and your petitions, in your newspaper advertisements and legal actions, and in your nights of prayer and fasting.

Hours and days have become months and years. Surely the road is very long. You each know your own personal, family, and community problems, which you bear along with you on the journey. But it is a journey shared in solidarity with our people and other peoples.

This is our framework of solidarity. It must grow until it is very broad, and to this end it is absolutely essential for the dispossessed to stay united. Communication and shared experiences will be the key to an activity network that will weave all our isolated labors together into one. Our network will then extend throughout a whole people. Our strength will wax great, for it will be the accumulated strength of many forces.

Let us, then, create concrete proposals. Let us take them to human rights organizations, to political parties, to commercial and professional groups, and to the church.

Of course, we shall be careful to respect the particular genius— the particular philosophy, organization, and manner of working —of each group to which we appeal. It is you yourselves who have urged us to do so. Such restraint is in itself indicative of your progress in working together in a common cause. Truly, unity is a precious commodity that is worth striving for at all costs.

CONCLUSIONS OF THE JULY 1980 MEETING OF THE PLAZA DE MAYO MOTHERS

Buenos Aires, July 20, 1980

A. *Immediate Objectives*

1. The demonstration set for August 14. Collect the members' signatures.

2. Distribution of the report of the Inter-American Commission on Human Rights of the Organization of American States.

3. Obtain office space and set up a headquarters.

4. Establish ties in greater Buenos Aires and the interior by expanding our ranks, creating local groups, and coordinating tasks.

5. Print our by-laws and the information bulletin on the Plaza de Mayo Mothers for distribution in the interior of the country. Issue a bi- or tri-lingual edition for other countries.

6. Maintain and strengthen ties with other countries. Essential travel to be undertaken with the participation of well-informed groups of mothers, taking advantage of relative geographical proximity, wherever possible.

7. Organize a meeting for the family members of mothers of missing persons. Invite competent professional people to this meeting to clarify situations of conflict and to advise on how to help the grandchildren, children, and parents of missing and imprisoned persons.

8. Prepare a document on the subject of No. 7 above for presentation by suitable prearrangement to the National Marian Congress that is to be held next October in Mendoza. Attend this Marian Congress to present our document.

9. Take up the question of moral and material assistance to needy families. Request the intervention of appropriate organizations.

10. Attend the meeting of the Task Force on Forced or Involuntary Disappearances (Resolution 20, section 36) of the United Nations Commission on Human Rights that is to be held in New York, September 15–19, 1980. Prepare notes and documentation for study by the Task Force. (Such information is to be received before August 15.)

11. Attend the sessions of the General Assembly of the Organization of American States that is scheduled to consider the Report of the Inter-American Commission on Human Rights concerned with Argentina. (Date and place to be arranged; probably the latter half of November in Lima or Washington.)

12. Make a presentation to the Vatican Synod that is to be held in October 1980. Emphasize the family and human rights.

13. Establish an emergency fund for unforeseen expenses.

14. Provide financial assistance to the group of grandmothers for their proposed newspaper advertisement.

15. Publish a declaration of solidarity with the people of Bolivia.

B. Short- and Medium-term Objectives

1. Strengthen relationships with political parties—not only with party leaders but also with the grassroots membership. Request party officials to schedule local meetings of their members and to hear and discuss the problem of the prisoners and missing. Try to get the parties to take a stand on this issue.

2. Do the same with the trade unions. Prepare lists of the prisoners and missing for each group we propose to visit.

3. Establish ties with student organizations and solicit their unofficial support.

4. Organize meetings like this one for the interior of the country.

5. Utilize available juridical avenues of approach by taking concrete legal action of various types.

6. Organize our work by setting up the following subcommittees, each to be comprised of five mothers: Aid and Assistance, Archives and Records, Coordination, External Relations, In-

ternal Relations, Greater Buenos Aires Relations, Translation (English, French, Italian, Portuguese), Press and Publicity, Work Pool. Elect a chairperson for each subcommittee. Involve as many of the mothers as possible in these subcommittees to avoid excessively burdening a few persons.

7. Publish a series of volumes entitled *Where Are They?*— with photographs, biographical data, details of arrest and disappearance, and efforts undertaken in his or her behalf for each prisoner and missing person. Write a single Introduction suitable for inclusion in each volume.

C. Long-term Objectives

1. Establish ties with similar organizations throughout the southern region.

2. Establish contacts with the European Common Market, the European Parliament, the International Labor Organization, UNESCO, the International Commission of Jurists, and other international organizations.

3. Organize our own group as a permanent pressure group for the defense of human rights.

4. Support the struggle for the dignity of human beings and for a response to their basic needs.

5. Familiarize the public with the National Constitution of 1853.

6. Avoid becoming the instrument of dominant ideologies or personalities.

7. Publish booklets containing available information on each prisoner and missing person, including photographs and statements by relatives and friends.

8. Strive for the historical vindication of the victims of repression.

D. Comments From the Final Debate

In view of the difficulties we have encountered in attempting to enter into contact with trade unions and professional organizations, we must establish ties with the families of workers who have been victimized by repression and with laborers who are already "conscientized" with respect to this problem.

Item. The subcommittees should not be great assemblies. It would be advisable to designate first the chairperson, who after due consultation would place in nomination the names of those persons she would like for her own subcommittee. Then all the mothers would vote on proposed subcommittee members at a later meeting. Several mothers have offered the use of their homes for subcommittee meetings.

Item. Our work shall be carried on in an organized rather than individualistic fashion.

Item. We will organize information chains for the orderly communication of matters of interest.

Item. It is recommended that some of us form teams of persons trained in the techniques of group dynamics to help ensure the orderly and effective conduct of our meetings and assemblies.

2.

The 150 Months of Resistance:
The "Snarlers" of the Perús
Cement Company

*The nonviolence of the "Mothers Courage" of the Argentine is
an appeal to human conscience as the ultimate norm of human
dignity. The nonviolence of Brazil's cement workers is a simple
appeal to law. We already have labor legislation, say these stubborn unionists. But it needs to be respected by the very state that
has created it.*

*First came a ninety-nine day strike. Then a 2,428-day legal bat-
tle for the reinstatement of 501 fired strikers. Finally, five years in
court over the equivalent of 20 million cruzeiros in back salaries.
It all added up to exactly 150 months of resistance to repression
and injustice from May 14, 1962 to November 14, 1974 in a battle
on two fronts: against the corruption of the judiciary by the employer, and against the sweetheart unionism of the Labor Ministry.*

*Such is the witness we see borne by members of an independent
union—the National Labor Front of São Paulo—with the help of
their attorney, Mario Carvalho de Jesús. It is a witness of "maintained fidelity," as they prefer to call it, a witness of active nonviolence in Brazil. It is the story of the Perús Cement Company
"snarlers," the nickname by which the workers compare themselves to wild boars brought to bay. Their story and their witness
have served ever since as a kind of basic reference work for the
nonviolent movement in Latin America. This is why Adolfo*

Pérez Esquivel tells that story all over the continent.

We now present the letter the snarlers wrote their fellow workers after the last legal battle was over.

MANIFESTO OF THE WORKERS OF PERÚS

Document published by the Permanent Committee of the Cement Workers' Union in November 1974 following the Labor Court decision requiring the Perús Cement Company to rehire more than 400 laborers and pay them seven years' back salary (some 20 million cruzeiros).

Fellow Workers of Perús!

Here are a few dates to remember:

May 14, 1962: Strike begins in collaboration with three other unions.

November 14, 1973: Official federal intervention begins for the second time.

November 14, 1974: Payment of back salaries begins.

A Reminder

On May 14, 1962, we began to fight side by side with three other unions representing Carioca Paper of São Paulo, Japy Textiles of Jundiaí, and Miranda Industries of Pirajuí, all companies of the Abdalla conglomerate. This was the date on which we submitted our list of special grievances for arbitration. Little did we suspect what we were letting ourselves in for! A twelve-and-a-half year battle—150 months of resistance to might and corruption!

Do you remember what our grievances were here at Perús?

1. We demanded to be paid on time. By May 14, 1962, we had not yet been paid for April.

2. We demanded payment of the production bonus to all workers in the factory. We had increased production by 450,000 bags in a period of a few months, but Mr. Abdalla was refusing to pay the bonus stipulated in the salary agreement imposed by the Regional Labor Court in October 1961.

3. We demanded that the company pay 10 percent of the health and disability insurance premium for all workers, as required by law.

4. We demanded the land that Mr. Abdalla was to have had subdivided so that each of us could build a home on our own plot, as provided in the bargaining agreement signed in 1960 and ratified by the Regional Labor Court. This land was ours by right: Mr. Abdalla had been withholding 5 percent of our monthly paycheck since October 1960 for these tracts. When at the request of the workers, the union committee demanded the land, Mr. Abdalla began his own construction on the land at Cajamar under false titles. After the start of the strike in 1962, Mr. Abdalla quickly attempted to rectify these criminal irregularities. But an investigation was held, and the Ministry of Public Affairs filed a fraud indictment. Thus the matter of our proprietorship of those tracts, on the basis of the 5 percent withholding of our pay, came before the courts. It had now been withdrawn from the Cajamar jurisdiction and transferred to the Appellate Division at Jundiaí.

5. We likewise demanded the payment of back wages to the employees of the São Paulo Cellulose Company, which was then in the process of constructing a plant at Gato Preto. The situation of these workers who belonged to our union was worse than our own situation.

6. Finally, we demanded the registration of some eighty members who were working on a eucalyptus plantation without benefit of either contract or day laborers' cards.

The Strike That Turned into a War

As we eventually learned, Mr. Abdalla provoked the strike himself. He wanted a strike. The "snarlers" had won a peaceful strike in 1958, and Mr. Abdalla had had to pay us for the forty-six days of the strike and give us a 40 percent pay hike besides. Now he wanted revenge. In fact, one month after the strike began on May 14, 1962, in collaboration with union members from three other factories whose situation was worse than our own, Mr. Abdalla negotiated a separate settlement with the officials of the other three unions—the paper and textile workers and the food handlers.

In an agreement signed (through the mediation of the president of the Federation of Food Handlers of São Paulo State, a known Communist), Mr. Abdalla acceded to the demands of all three unions. Actually, however, *two agreements* were signed on that occasion. Only one was for publication and would be used in concluding the hearing. The other was marked "Confidential"—a secret agreement—and its terms were not to be divulged to the workers in the three plants. But we managed to obtain a copy of it, signed by the president of the Miranda Workers' Union, and we included it in the dossier we prepared for our own hearing on Mr. Abdalla's unwarranted firing of 501 senior workers [workers with at least ten years' seniority, as verified by regular federal inspection] (Case No. 1752/62 of the Appellate Division). And so we were able to demonstrate to the Labor Court that Mr. Abdalla had discriminated against the "snarlers" in order to try to bring them to their knees. Mr. Abdalla had transformed the strike into a war. He was a deputy at the time, and could count on state and federal support from the politicians, not to mention the police.

As everyone knows, and as we have reported to the São Paulo authorities time and again, for more than fifteen years the personnel director of the Abdalla conglomerate has been a retired police chief, and the police headquarters at Cajamar have always been in one of Mr. Abdalla's buildings.

The Labor Court Does Its Duty

The first decision handed down by the Labor Court was against us. We later learned the reason for this miscarriage of justice: the judge and Mr. Abdalla were in cahoots. Standards were not as strict in the Labor Court in 1962 as they are today. There was no selection by lot. The chronological order of deposition of grievances was not observed. This was the heyday of the "finaglers," as they were called. People could have a trial assigned to any judge they chose. And, of course, Mr. Abdalla is a first-class finagler.

We lost our case before the Conciliation and Judgment Commission by two to one. The Commissioner for the Workers dissented in our favor. But as most of us came to realize in the course of the trial (there were a dozen sessions), the presiding commissioner was grossly partial. Our attorney and Dr. Cesarino both protested repeatedly, as can be seen from the record of the proceedings.

But "truth will win out" if you persevere, and the presiding judge was eventually suspended and removed from the bench. (He then became Mr. Abdalla's "private attorney," and this is what he is today.)

The Executive Branch Begins to Do Its Duty

All these things were reported in the papers as they occurred: the *Estado de São Paulo*, the *Jornal da Tarde*, *Notícias Populares*, *Jornal do Brasil*, *O Globo*, and the weekly *São Paulo*. Then besides the papers, two books carried our story: We published *The Perús Strike Comes to Court* in 1967 in collaboration with thirty-three unions of São Paulo and ten workers' federations of São Paulo State. Our "little green book," *The Perús Case and Union Liberty in Brazil,* appeared in 1974 under the auspices of the Permanent Commission of Perús Workers (representing the "snarlers") and the National Labor Front.

In the "little green book" we printed the petition we had signed along with our friends of Perús and Cajamar (priests, ministers, teachers, university students, workers in other industries, and others) and members of our families—more than 3,500 signatures in all. This petition was sent to President Ernesto Geisel, who in July 1974 decided to establish an interministerial commission with the task of studying some of the problems of the Abdalla conglomerate. The commission was to be weighted in Mr. Abdalla's favor by omitting certain key officials who would otherwise have been on it. The problems to be handled by the commission were, as we recalled in our petition, five in number:

1. Seizure of the goods and chattels of the Perús Cement Company, so that, as a result, the factory becomes the property of the union.

2. Payment of salaries due of upwards of 20,000,000 cruzeiros to more than four hundred workers or their heirs.

3. Discontinuance of administrative intervention in union affairs.

4. Withdrawal of Socal from Cajamar and the expropriation of the quarries allotted to Perne for exploration after approval by all Socal workers, who are then to be transferred back to Perús.

5. Finally, it is recognized that the Receivership Commission [which was then managing Perús under federal auspices] is performing yeoman's service, increasing production by 30 percent and contracting with a filtration company for the installation of antipollution equipment. But this commission is forced to work with a number of senior members of the old management staff who are interfering with its effectiveness. We are convinced that pollution in the area will cease now that the cement factory is under federal administration.

On October 24, 1974, the first anniversary of the dismissal of our union attorney, President Geisel finally settled the Socal affair by signing the bill to seize Perús and the Perús and Pirapora Railroad. In so doing, he definitively removed the Perús Cement Company from Mr. Abdalla's control and ensured the cessation of pollution in the region.

On November 14, 1974, the first anniversary of the current administrative intervention in our union affairs, we began to receive our back wages.

Thus the only outstanding grievance is the one concerning official interference in union affairs. Patience! All things come to those who wait.

The Price We Paid for the Strike

As we have indicated, it was Mr. Abdalla who managed to transform a simple strike that was considered legal by the Labor Court into an out-and-out war. No amount of money can ever repay us for the hardships that war entailed for us. No one struck Perús for the money we are starting to receive twelve and one-half years later. It is the largest amount the Labor Court could have awarded; but it is a modest sum indeed in view of the fact that we are senior employees who never drew on the Unemployment Fund [established by federal law in 1969 to provide compensation in case of involuntary termination].

However, the strike that turned into a war had its plus side, too. It provided a number of valuable lessons:

1. It is of no use for the employer to count on police intimidation—arrests, threats, billy clubbings, and accusations—when workers keep a cool head, stay within the letter of the law, and refuse to succumb to provocations to violence. Every police investigation was ordered closed by the independent Ministry of Public Affairs. No one was found guilty of anything.

2. Together workers can win what is legally theirs—or even a bit more, as when we won the Living Wage Agreement in 1959, three years ahead of anybody else in the labor force. Separately, workers are afraid to complain to their unions or even to the Labor Court. Private grievances are a risky business. You can lose your job.

3. In spite of two administrative interventions—from 1964 to 1965 and from 1973 to the present—the workers have been able to maintain their unity and organization. The inspector managed to get his hands on our union, but not on our consciences.

4. In as much as the purpose of law is to punish the guilty, you can count on our system of justice (once it wins its own independence). It found Mr. Abdalla guilty of cutting off the electricity in our homes in 1965 and of threatening Dr. Milton and pressuring him not to testify on our behalf in the open hearing before the Labor Court. Dr. Milton did his duty anyway, independent and honorable person that he is, and went to court and made his deposition. In reprisal he was dismissed from Perús. That is a crime, and for that crime Mr. Abdalla has already gone to jail. He is currently under two further indictments as well—one at Jundiaí for fraud and embezzlement of that 5 percent of our wages for the subdivision, and another criminal indictment before the Lower Federal Court in São Paulo in connection with the arraignment of the Perús and Socal Board of Directors. In this last case there are already seventy depositions in the dossier by victims and witnesses; the first hearing is scheduled for January 1975.

5. Our denunciation since 1958 of the crimes and offenses of the Abdalla conglomerate finally induced the government to act with firmness and resolve and to seize several of Mr. Abdalla's

factories and buildings. It wasn't easy! But it shows that "God may take his time, but he always gets there."

6. We experienced over the years a real solidarity with members of other unions as well as with university students, intellectuals, the Catholic church (97 percent of it at any rate), and our Protestant friends.

7. We learned that we could hold out and win in the end even when a number of us weakened and actually went so far as to grant power of attorney to Mr. Abdalla's private counsel for the purpose of a deposition against officials of the union, officers of the Cajamar Community Association, and our own attorney! We put up with all of this very patiently. Today some of these same union members whom Mr. Abdalla used so shamefully are "snarlers" once more. In fact, two of them have just rejoined us—after learning that the money for their back wages is lying on the desk in the Labor Court! Patience. Every group has its weak members. Christ himself knew a traitor and the weakness of Saint Peter.

8. We proved that workers can hold out. We held a ninety-nine day strike from May 24 to August 21, 1962, and then waged a legal battle that went through twelve separate decisions. The Labor Court is slow. The executive branch fails to provide the needed judges. But the delay is partly balanced out by the money award. We waited 2,428 days to go back to work—and twelve and one-half years to collect our paychecks.

9. We proved that workers' power of resistance is greater when they can count on the support of their families at home. Of course, we had this support only because our resistance was peaceful. There were no brawls. Not a single factory window was broken. We wept with rage, many of us, as we fought off the temptation to "let 'em have it." But if you look at the facts, you see that what really counts is not being brave just now and then. What counts is being brave all the time—all your life long if you have to. This is our approach. We call it "steadfastness," or "maintained fidelity"—standing our ground. It is the "violence of the peaceful" begun by Christ, continued by the apostles, and experienced during the first three centuries of Christianity. Later, Christians became lax and conservative, nearly all of them, until

Gandhi rediscovered "nonviolence," as it is usually called. We think the term "nonviolence" is weak. We prefer to call it "maintained fidelity."

10. We showed that "snarlers" harbor no resentment; they can forget offenses and insults. We proved that we are workers who know how to fulfill our obligations and assert our rights. After the cement factory was seized, production went up 30 percent. We know that work well done gives human beings an interior freedom. Our conscience tells us very clearly when we are doing right and when we are doing wrong. The "snarlers" always try to do right. We try to do right by our comrades, our families, and the society we have an obligation to improve.

Our Commitment to the Junior Workers

We are setting aside 10 percent of our award for the junior workers [the some three hundred workers discharged with less than ten years' seniority who did not share in the Labor Court's award to the 501 "senior workers"] as well as to repay our attorney in some small way for his personal contribution to our strike effort (the use of his house, a 1,500 sq. m. plot of ground, his garage, and his car). We know that this is very little. As we have stated, nobody struck Perús for the money. Double this amount would still be too little. For us, just going back to work, back to the factory, in 1969 was a victory. Remember? Back to work, that and nothing more. But it was a great victory for the working class, as we have seen in the ten points listed above—the ten things we learned in the course of twelve and a half years of battling.

By setting aside 10 percent, we are trying to show that what we are doing is a bit different from what people do when they talk about solidarity but fail to match their words with deeds. We shall never forget that our junior comrades-in-arms unaccountably lost their big case (whereas they won another one in the same Labor Court). Strange things happen. As we know, human justice is far from perfect. People all have their failings and weaknesses.

Our 10 percent is meant to be a symbol. As a symbol, it may actually represent more than the legal compensation the juniors would have received had they won their case. The God who guided us down this whole long road will know how to help us find a solution that is not just financial.

The Union

As we have seen, four of our original grievances have been remedied by the government. One remains: the return of our union local, which we created ourselves and which should remain in our hands. The workers are perfectly capable of selecting their own officials. If they make a mistake, they can remove unworthy officials from office, as provided in the union charter. Everyone knows the battle is easier or not quite so hard when you have a union on your side. But when people in your own local are in bed with your employer, there is not much you can do. In that case it is better to leave home and camp out in the open with comrades who have not sold themselves to the company.

Administrative intervention in union activities has been going on for a year now, and the labor inspection has produced no results. Patience. All things come to those who wait. In fact, we think the administrative intervention, while a serious error on the part of the Labor Ministry, has demonstrated that the fight can be fought with just a "people union"—without the "paper union" of the nine-to-five clerks who close up shop nights and weekends when the workers have time to use their local headquarters. Obviously they are taking orders from somebody else, not from us. We do not intend to forget that we have repeatedly requested authorization from the labor inspector for a meeting in our local offices with our attorney—even if intervention officials have to be present—and he has always refused.

Again, the administrative intervention in the union is unjustified. It has only hurt us and helped Mr. Abdalla. It is an arbitrary and unjustified act. It is in contravention of the agreements signed by Brazil with the International Labor Organization in Geneva in Europe. Mr. Abdalla is a well-known lawbreaker. He is the greatest scofflaw in the world.

Crime calls for punishment. We have exhausted every avenue of recourse with the administrative intervention. So now we have decided to lodge a complaint against the government of Brazil itself with the International Labor Organization. We have the right to demand that the government take all necessary measures to discipline officials who make a mockery of the law and are partial to Mr. Abdalla. All this is explained in our pamphlet *The Perús Case and Union Liberty in Brazil*. The administrative intervention must be terminated. Nothing can go on forever.

An Alarm

Note well, fellow workers, these two points:

1. Our co-workers from Socal must join the union. No one is going to be fired for doing so. "Super Snoop" is gone; he is in the dock himself now. In a few months elections will be held. You will be able to vote for the union officials of your choice.

2. Those of you who are retired or on sick leave have the same rights as those who are on the job, even if you are not paying your dues. The only exception is that you cannot be elected as officials. But you can vote. Here the law is a good one. Stick close to your union locals. Elections are just around the corner. ("All things come to those who wait.") We shall be able to choose our own leaders, and that will be a fine thing, indeed.

Be sure to come and vote. We are about to put an end to the "sweetheart unionism" about which everybody complains and which is still in excellent health.

A Request

Every one of us has a story to tell. It is a story of twelve and one-half years of resistance, a story of ourselves, our families, and our struggle with management and government. Tell us that story. Write it out and send it in. Recall at least two things that happened: one on the hard side—the sad side—and the other on the happy side. If you are not comfortable writing, get one of your children or neighbors to help you, or ask one of us on the Permanent Committee. Write very plainly and frankly, and as much as you like. The committee will summarize your letters in a book. We need your help. You have thirty days; please send us your story.

Two Questions

Please send us your answers to these questions:

1. After such a long and painful struggle, will it perhaps be worthwhile to hold a meeting with our fellow workers in junior status and with everyone who has helped us through these twelve and a half years (from May 14, 1962 to November 14, 1974)? Please tell us what you think about this in writing within five days of receiving your back pay.

2. Is May 14, 1962, a "Day to Remember"? Is it a day we should never forget or ever let our children forget? Should we meet every year on this date at union headquarters or perhaps in the street outside? Please answer in writing within five days.

A Friendly Warning

We made it. People are going to think it's all so wonderful. Watch out, you're going to be drowning in bouquets. But this is no time for the "snarlers" to strut. Talk about the strike every chance you have. Tell everybody what happened. Tell it just as you recall it. Use the pages to spark your memory. Let's show the world we know a way to grow, inwardly as human beings. Let's show them how they can win a fight without hatred or underhandedness. A person can grow as a human being by defending truth and justice. A person can grow as a human being by learning to distinguish between people and their acts. Sometimes we have to teach our children a lesson because we love them. We have to try to bring them back to the straight and narrow. This is the way it is with Abdalla. We mean him no harm. He has a family too, just as we have, and we respect his family. He is going to be punished. And, of course, he should be. He will learn a lesson now; he will amend his ways. This is all the "snarlers" want. We just want everyone to become better, little by little and day by day, and to grow inwardly—and without any brown-nosing.

We are all members of one family, yesterday, today, and tomorrow. We know we shall find peace only where we find justice—only where we find respect for all human beings, only where all human beings have the right to a decent living for themselves and their families.

Forward, snarlers! The battle is never won! United we stand. If people do not like what we do, that is only to be expected. It is something we have to talk over with them. We are willing to reconsider our positions. We are willing to change anything that we may be doing wrong. We only ask for goodwill from others in all frankness and honesty. Today I help my comrade; tomorrow my comrade will help me. And not just with money or material things, either. The word of a friend and comrade when the going gets rough is worth more than all the money in the world.

We are waiting for your written replies. We need them.

The Permanent Committee of Perús Workers

Sebastião Fernandes Cruz, João Breno Pinto,
Ivambergue Suzart Machado, Gino Resaghi,
Oscar Gondari Wurzbacher, Reinaldo Pessini,
Mário Carvalho de Jesús, Attorney-at-Law

Frente Nacional do Trabalho
Avenida Ipiranga, 1267, Ninth Floor
São Paulo

3.

Torment on the Plateau: The Indians' Story

Ecuador, 1973. The Indians of the community of Toctezinín in the Province of Chimborazo learn that, as sharecroppers on a huge domain, they can now become proprietors of the land they work. The Agrarian Reform Law has just been amended to this effect by the progressive government of General Rodríguez Lara.

But what can the right of little peasants—Indians, at that —matter to those who, as the prophet Isaiah put it long ago, ". . . add house to house and join field to field until everywhere belongs to them and they are the sole inhabitants of the land" (Isa. 5:8)?

When the military police fired on the people of Toctezinín on September 26, 1974, and killed Lázaro Conto, it took all of Bishop Leonidas Proaño's faith to be able to stand at the Indian's coffin, face the crowd, and cry, "Lazarus, rise, come forth!"

But this is just the kind of strength the world's poor possess. These are the poor of the Bible, and they have the strength to believe, in spite of all threats and blackmail, that they will obtain justice. This is what the Indians of Toctezinín wrote to the president of the Republic of Ecuador. Their faith in the God of the gospel inspires them to resist oppression and spoliation. The solidarity of the evangelist of nonviolence, Bishop Proaño, the support of the pastoral team of the province of Chimborazo, and the encouragement of Pérez Esquivel's Service of Peace and Justice— all these persons and groups invest the struggle of the people for

71

justice and dignity with a scope that encompasses all of Latin America. Their struggle serves as an example to be imitated by all who suffer humiliation.

OPEN LETTER FROM THE INDIANS OF TOCTEZINÍN

Our Indian Community of Toctezinín in the commune of Chunchi, Chimborazo Province, is seven years old. It is recognized by the Labor Ministry and the Department of Welfare.

When the Deputy Minister of Labor came to help celebrate our community's official inauguration, he sent us in search of common lands we could hold collectively. We could build a school there, he said, and plant our crops. That was seven years ago. We have still not found our common lands.

There are eighty-five of us here in the community, all working as sharecroppers on large farms nearby. One of these farms is the Magna estate, and some of its fields are the cause of all our trouble.

Here is how it happened. Four years ago, Mercedes Murillo de Yerovi, one of the heirs of the late proprietor of Magna, Leopoldo Murillo, leased part of the old estate—tracts known as Almidón—to Amalia Merchán de Velasteguí. Twenty-four of us then went to work for Mrs. Merchán as sharecroppers or tenants. We cleared all the land ourselves, and farmed it for three years. Mrs. Merchán contributed no assistance of any kind. These were virgin lands. We provided the labor, seed, teams, and tools. We even had to transport our harvest to the roadbed.

Mrs. Merchán likewise employed us in her own personal fields, paying us six or seven sucres a day the first year, eight the second, and ten the third, for a task that at harvest time lasts from dawn till dusk.

After three years we learned that a land reform proposal had been voted in favor of the peasants. So we held a meeting, and as a result of the meeting sent our community council in a body on December 14, 1973, to visit the district offices of the Ecuadorian Institute of Agrarian Reform and Colonization (IERAC), asking them to send someone to tell our community what our rights were and how to go about getting them. The district director instructed us to continue to farm Almidón, but as sharecroppers no longer. Now we were to keep the whole harvest for ourselves.

Thus in January 1974 we began to do our farming according to the instructions received from IERAC. There is no doubt that IERAC intended us to proceed in this way—the district director instructed the communal manager (the Chunchi town manager) to guarantee our ownership of Almidón.

But Mrs. Merchán, who is on good terms with the police commissioner and his officers (the commissioner's wife is Mrs. Merchán's cousin), sent the commissioner and his people into our fields to threaten us and interfere with our work. By now there were about sixty of us. We had asked our neighbors for help in the planting since now the harvest was to belong to the whole community.

This is when the national commissioner at Chunchi referred us once more to the district director at Riobamba. So sixteen of us formed a delegation and made the trip. There in the IERAC offices we met with Mrs. Murillo and Mrs. Merchán. Their attorney, Francisco Oleas, was there, and so was ours, Alfredo Parra. We asked Mrs. Murillo to sell us—not give us, but sell us—the acreage we had been working. But she replied that she preferred to sell it to Mrs. Merchán. At this point the director of the IERAC district proposed a compromise. The Indian community would take one side of the property and Mrs. Merchán the other, instead of our fields and hers lying helter-skelter as before. After all, the road splits the land in two—we could take one side, and Mrs. Merchán could have the other. This was agreed to, and the director recommended that we all simply continue to work our land, our newly assigned fields, "until such time as an official decision could be rendered in the matter." The director's plan allotted us less land than we had requested, but we accepted it all the same.

Then in January as we were working our fields, Lt. Col. Zumárraga, the governor, rode into Almidón on horseback to examine the condition of the fields. When his inspection was over, he divided up the tracts of the domain, assigning the ones below the road to Mrs. Merchán, and those above it to us, the Indians. Then he instructed all parties to plant and harvest their newly assigned fields "until the matter could be officially settled."

Mrs. Merchán, however, had other ideas. She held to her intention to purchase the whole Almidón estate herself without any regard for our rights and to register it all in her name alone. We repeatedly protested this proposal to IERAC through our community council, especially in March when we first learned about it. Here again the district director came to our defense. On March 21 he sent a memorandum to the national commissioner at Chunchi, asking him to certify our title. On April 5 the district commissioner sent another memorandum to the town clerk at Chunchi, asking him not to record any deed of sale to Mrs. Merchán because the recording of all property-transfer deeds was prohibited by law until regulations could be published for property transfers.

But no satisfaction was forthcoming. Both memoranda were ignored. So we lodged another protest with the district director of IERAC, and this time he wrote a memorandum to the town manager at Chunchi, our communal manager, expressing surprise that his other notes had had no effect, in particular the one asking for certification of our title to the land. Ever since May Mrs. Merchán had repeatedly declared that we were to deliver to her the landholder's share of our harvest as if we were still only sharecroppers on this land that had been assigned to us by the governor and by IERAC. In addition, Mrs. Merchán began through one of her employees to spread certain rumors about "the Indians."

And this brings us to the events of the past two weeks.

On Wednesday, July 17, a group of us were working in the fields in volunteer details, clearing the irrigation ditches. Suddenly we received a summons to the office of the communal manager, Heriberto Castro. Mrs. Merchán's employee who brought us the message (the same employee who had spread the rumors about us at Mrs. Merchán's behest) told us that the reason for the summons was to accompany the communal manager to the bank on business. Thus our comrades, Rodolfo Lema, president of the Indian community, Ricardo Tamay, justice of the peace and president of Richarimui [the Indian Awareness Movement] in Chimborazo Province, Manuel Pérez, and Asunción Lema went to the town hall. There the communal manager was waiting for them, all right, but so were the police. The communal manager advised them that on July 5, after a work detail like the one we had been on that day, they had been heard singing and uttering insults against the authorities of the commune and province and even of the federal government. Our comrades were jailed on the spot.

The next day they were transferred to the house of correction in Riobamba, where they were sentenced to seven days in jail and a fine of 240 sucres. Officials later told us that the accusation against them had originated with the chief of police in Chunchi, and that its terms were similar to those used by the communal manager. The denunciation itself had been made by our neighbor, José María Tamay, Mrs. Merchán's friend and a faithful partisan of her cause.

The accusations were false. Indeed our comrades had been singing after the work detail was completed. But they had insulted no one, least of all the authorities. In fact, Rodolfo Lema had not even been with them. José María Tamay and José Procel had therefore perjured themselves. (Another youth, one Telmo Rumisaca, declined to give false testimony, despite the fact that he was threatened with a beating if he refused to do so. Thus our five friends had to spend seven days in jail. (Thanks to the intervention of our attorney, the bishop, and our pastor, however, the fine was suspended.)

Our comrades were released on July 23. But as the new governor was away for the day, they had to return on Friday, July 26, for a meeting with him. Present at the meeting were Mrs. Merchán, the chief of police, and José María Tamay. The governor now attempted to coerce the five into signing an agreement according to which the Indian community would share with Mrs. Merchán, just as if we were still sharecroppers, the potatoes we had been planting for three years in the fields now leased to her by Mrs. Murillo—even though every part of the effort itself was ours alone, both seed and labor, and even though this year, in accordance with the verbal authorization we had received from IERAC, the whole harvest was to have been ours. As for Almidón, where we had planted beans, the governor demanded that we turn over one quarter of our harvest to Mrs. Merchán. After the harvest we were to abandon the fields for good. In other words we were to be evicted from our lands.

Of course, this arrangement was altogether contrary to the instructions given by the previous governor, Lt. Col. Zumárraga, as well as by IERAC in Riobamba. The new governor, Américo Alava, explained that Mrs. Merchán now held a land title delivered by the main office of IERAC in Quito. And after all, he asked, who were we to complain, seeing that Mrs. Merchán had now paid us 12,500 sucres in embezzled back salaries as required of her by the Riobamba Labor Court? (Of course, in law these two matters are juridically discreet.)

But our five comrades, Rodolfo Lema, Ricardo Tamay, Humberto Marcantoma, Gilberto Loja, and Hilário Guaman, refused to renounce the rights that were ours by law. And so they were thrown into jail once more "until further notice" for "rebellion" and what the governor called "gross and vulgar conduct."

Yesterday, July 31, was the sixth day of their new jail term. Today is the seventh day, but they have not as yet been released. We have learned that still another sentence has been imposed upon them, but try as we may, we cannot learn anything more.

We believe that we are the victims of an injustice. Were the accusations lodged against us and our companions true, this treatment would be just and merited, and we would accept it. We only ask that the law be observed, and that our right to purchase our fields at a just price be respected.

We have come here today to beg the help of other Indian communities. Our homes and our fields are going to ruin. Our wives and children have nothing left to eat.

But we shall continue to fight. We act in disrespect of no one, but we will obtain justice.

The Indian Community of Toctezinín

August 1, 1974

LETTER TO THE PRESIDENT OF ECUADOR

Toctezinín, September 13, 1974

General Guillermo Rodríguez Lara
President of the Republic of Ecuador
Quito

Dear Mr. President:

Cordial greetings from the Indian people of the community of Toctezinín. We are writing to you because you are the only one who can help. The authorities of our commune turn a deaf ear to our pleas, and those of the province are even less willing to listen. All ignore our sufferings and the problems we are having with our land. The authorities say they will "straighten out the situation of the peasants." Instead, they harrass us with false denunciations and false interpretations of our acts, so as to keep the peasantry in the same demeaning subjection as before. They do not answer us. Indeed, they do not even allow us to speak. When an agreement is being drawn up between any two parties, the authorities refuse to let the country folk speak up and tell their side. They will not leave us in peace. They terrorize us with their weapons, their rifles, and their threats, and with what they call "tear-gas bombs," which make people lose consciousness. The authorities have a clique. If they are truly the "authorities," why do they take orders from Mrs. Merchán?

We have respected and complied with all the dispositions of the outgoing governor, as well as with the instructions we have received from our district IERAC. We only ask that we be respected too.

Now the problem is that harvest time has come. Never has Mrs. Merchán made any contribution to our work, and yet suddenly she claims an authority superior to that of the governor himself by demanding that we share our harvest with her and then leave the land. We received no help from her whatever. She did not even give us seed. The authorities are simply refusing to carry out the orders of the district IERAC and the former governor. We suppose that when the present governor is replaced, his successor will say something else, and the one who comes next will have still another opinion. We no longer know where to turn to find the competent authority to resolve our problem. Our leaders are asked to make contracts that the people oppose or know nothing about. We are informed that we shall continue to be arrested, and that we shall be sent off to the Oriente Rain Forest—the police will come to our homes and herd us and our wives and our children into trucks and just drive away.

You are the father of your people. We hope that we shall obtain justice by your intervention. We wish no violence among the brothers and sisters of your family, and we are ready to die if need be, if only you will do us justice.

We are a people of solidarity, we peasants, and our solidarity extends to all who, like us, are victims of threats and beatings. But when we go to make a complaint, our deposition is refused.

You see, Mr. President, we live in a region of the country where there is still oppression. We are surrounded by the great estates. But we are a juridically recognized community: we farm our land collectively for the common welfare. We live as many as twelve to a house, and if they take our fields we shall have nowhere to go.

The whole trouble is a lack of official regulations. As if our problems were not serious enough already, now they have cut off our water supply, the only source we had available. If we Indians dared to go to town for water, it would be different. But they keep arresting us in town. The enclosed documents will show you what we mean.

Right now the president and secretary of our community are in Quito, doing what they can for us themselves, and so their signatures are missing here. We thank you in advance, Mr. President, for your kind attention and prompt reply. We know we can count on you for justice.

GOD, COUNTRY, AND FREEDOM

Respectfully yours,

For the Toctezinín Community,

Porfirio Pérez
Vice President

Floresmilo Marcantoma
Treasurer

[Sig. illegible]
Trustee

SOLIDARITY WITH THE INDIANS IN THEIR HOUR OF AGONY

Statement issued by Bishop Proaño of Riobamba after the events of September 26, 1974, that led to the murder of Lázaro Condo and the detention of other persons who had been working in the Indians' cause.

To All Persons Who Have Regard for Truth and Justice:

1. In the matter of the arrest and imprisonment of the vicar general of the Diocese of Riobamba, the Reverend Augustín Emilio Bravo, and thirty other persons, the minister of state has declared:

> According to earliest reports, this was a matter of the eviction of peasants, not of the violation of a sacred place. . . . The National Guard acted on orders from Chimborazo Province authorities and in strict accordance with the dispositions of the law. . . . The same procedure will continue to be employed in all similar instances. At a moment when our country must increase its farm output . . . it would scarcely seem appropriate for the government to countenance the fomenting of anarchy by private interest groups in utter disregard of proper legal procedures.[3]

2. Confronted as we are with the occurrences of this Thursday, September 26—referred to by the minister of state in the declaration reported above—and the interpretation by the same minister with regard to the detention of the vicar general of the Diocese of Riobamba and thirty other persons, we deem ourselves under the obligation to elucidate the whole truth of the matter, clearly and concisely, *for all persons who have any regard for truth and justice.*

3. The members of the Indian community of Toctezinín have worked as sharecroppers, that is, as tenants, on estates surrounding their community. One of these estates is the Magna property, which belonged to the late Leopoldo Murillo. Among Mr. Murillo's heirs is a certain Mercedes Murillo de Yerovi; the part of the Murillo estate falling to her is called "Almidón." Mrs. Murillo leased this land to Amalia Merchán de Velasteguí. A good part of the Toctezinín community began to work as sharecroppers for Mrs. Merchán four years ago.

4. In view of the provisions of the Agrarian Reform Law, the Indian community of Toctezinín decided to send representatives to the district offices of IERAC in Riobamba; on the occasion of

this visit, the director of the Riobamba district of IERAC autho-
rized the Indians to continue to farm their land *as with title of
possession and no longer as sharecroppers.* On the basis of this
authorization the members of the community began their January planting this year.

5. In support of this authorization and in order to facilitate its
implementation, the IERAC director of the Riobamba district
addressed three memoranda to the national commissioner at
Chunchi—on February 12, March 21, and March 30, 1974—requesting the national commissioner to "take the necessary
measures to *maintain the existing state of proprietorship"* (em-
phasis ours) so that "each person can continue to work the same
fields in the same way as heretofore free of all lets and hin-
drances."

6. Subsequent to a written complaint filed by the president of
the Toctezinín community to the effect that a contract of sale had
been signed between the proprietor and the lessee, the IERAC
director of the Riobamba district addressed an official communication to the town clerk at Chunchi, informing him that "even
though this instrument [the contract of sale] were to bear the authorization of the executive director of IERAC, it cannot be admitted as a document having any effect in law." The director
added:

> Accordingly, I now request you to refrain from recording
> any deed whereby the party attempting to sell may pretend
> to confer rights and prerogatives with respect to the Magna
> estate upon the party attempting to buy *inasmuch as all
> property transfer is in suspense until such time as regula-
> tions concerning the Agrarian Reform may be promulgated*
> [emphasis ours].

7. As the repeated instructions of the IERAC director of the
Riobamba district concerning the maintenance of the existing
state of proprietorship continued to go unheeded, the same district director then addressed an official note to the communal
manager of Chunchi. The manager was requested:

> . . . [to] intervene in this matter to protect the existing state
> of proprietorship with respect to said domain; that is, let

each one in possession and working the land continue to work in the same way until such time as may IERAC intervene directly after the regulations for the implementation of the Agrarian Reform Law have been promulgated.

8. The authorities of Chunchi not only failed to comply with the dispositions emanating from the Riobamba district of IERAC but, in connivance with the lessee and with the encouragement of the provincial authorities, they also unleashed a flood of repression and threats against members of the Toctezinín community. Their intent was clearly to intimidate them and force them to sign a sharecroppers' contract containing a clause whereby they would also be evicted from their fields. On July 17 of this year, Rodolfo Lema, president of the community, Ricardo Tamay, justice of the peace, and two members of the same community, Manuel Pérez and Asunción Lema, were sentenced to seven days in jail and a fine of 240 soles. On July 26, after a meeting at the office of the governor with Mrs. Amalia Merchán, the communal manager of Chunchi, and five officials of the Toctezinín community, the latter were sentenced to a further seven days in jail, this time for having declined to affix their signatures to the agreement accepting sharecroppers' status and eviction from the fields. Thus they had not even completed their sentences when they were sentenced again—once more to seven days in jail.

Upon the occasion of these jailings, I applied in writing both to the governor of the province and the commanding officer in charge of the police, requesting to be informed of "the causes for which said farmers have been arrested and confined." I received no reply. On the same occasion I held personal meetings with the two above-mentioned authorities, seeking a comprehensive, just resolution of the matter—but again without any result. Meanwhile, armed police officers, accompanied by Mrs. Amalia Merchán and her retainers, paid frequent visits to the Toctezinín community for the purpose of insulting, threatening, and intimidating the people. The intent of these acts was to induce them to sign the agreement on their sharecroppers' status and on their eviction from the land. It would be impossible to list here the entire series of acts of intimidation carried out at this time.

9. In view of these demeaning acts, the officials of Toctezinín made application directly to the minister of state. They prevailed

upon Undersecretary of State Dr. Carlos Estarellas Merino to dispatch a telegram to the communal manager of Chunchi in the following terms:

> Kindly desist once for all from harassing members of the Toctezinín community. If any member is detained, inform me about the terms of the accusation, the place, and the reason for the arrest, and send me a copy of report, as required by the regulations.

The Indians likewise persuaded the coordinator general of the Ministry of State to direct a communication to the military governor of Chimborazo, summarizing the farmers' grievances and requesting the governor:

> . . . to order an inquiry into the conduct of said official [the communal manager] as a result of direct and repeated requests made to this ministry by the peasants themselves, who complain of the terror inspired in this section of the population and of the reprisals they fear may be visited upon them by the said communal manager.

In addition, the Indians' further prevailed upon the IERAC land officer to send a communication to the IERAC director of the Riobamba district, informing him that members of the community of Toctezinín had applied to IERAC for a "guarantee of their proprietary rights to these lands." This communication closed in the following terms:

> On the strength of what I have just recounted, I ask you, Mr. District Director, to be so good as to intervene with the governor of Chimborazo Province in Riobamba. Please continue to display your customary zeal in coordinating the efforts of your service and those of the governor in carrying out the agrarian laws touching on the rights demanded by the Indian community.

10. The pastoral team of Chunchi, faithful to its commitments to the poor and the oppressed, has been most concerned about

forming basic ecclesial communities, both in towns and the countryside. This pastoral endeavor has aroused the hostility of large landholders and other persons accustomed to exploiting the peasantry. As a result, the pastoral team of Chunchi has been the target of various kinds of attacks and assaults. On July 7 one of its members was ambushed and beaten. On August 25 two of its members were the victims of an armed assault. Stones are continuously cast at windows in the rectory. At daybreak threats and insults are shouted in the road before the rectory. Insults and death threats are made by Mrs. Amalia Merchán in the offices of local authorities, in the streets, and in public busses. All these attacks have been duly reported to the local and provincial authorities, who have made no effort whatever to guarantee the safety or to protect the lives of members of the pastoral team. Because of the absence of official cooperation, other ministerial teams of the diocese have taken turns for several days at a time in accompanying the Chunchi pastoral team on its daily rounds.

11. In accord with the above-cited IERAC authorization, members of the Indian community decided to begin harvesting their crops on September 25. To this purpose they solicited the cooperation of members of other farm communities. The first day's work went forward without incident. But on the morning of Thursday, September 26, 1974, according to information received from the peasants themselves, the harvesters were suddenly surrounded by detachments of soldiers and armed police accompanied by Messrs. Jorge Bermeo, Luis Ordóñez, Gilberto Ordóñez, and two or three other residents of Chunchi. The soldiers demanded to know by what authority the peasants were harvesting the crops. The latter responded that they were doing so on the authority of IERAC's Riobamba district. Ignoring this reply, the National Guard detachment that had been dispatched to the premises began to strike the peasants, dealing blows to both men and women and forcing them into waiting vehicles by striking them with their fists and the butts of their rifles. The soldiers and police told the peasants that their orders were to "shoot to kill." Indeed, when some of the peasants attempted to flee, the soldiers began to fire on them, probably at this time wounding one of the peasants in the stomach and head.

According to information furnished by several of the peasants, it seems the victim was a farmer named Lázaro Condo, who has died. For members of his community no longer have any news about him. An unknown number of others were also wounded during the incident. In these circumstances some twenty farmers were arrested and taken to Riobamba Prison.

12. A little earlier on that same morning, a detachment of soldiers surrounded the rectory at Chunchi. In order to gain entrance to the rectory, they profaned the church, breaking down the interior doors beneath the belfry that connect the church to the rectory. Once inside, they began arresting everyone they met, including Father Augustín Emilio Bravo, vicar general of the diocese, and Gustavo Loza, a layman. Both men had arrived the evening before in order to accompany the pastor to Riobamba. This was at my instruction, since I had learned the night before that the pastor's health was very precarious. His already delicate diabetic condition had been aggravated as a result of the tension under which he had been forced to live. This explains the presence of the vicar general on the premises. The peasants as well as all the others arrested at this time were held strictly incommunicado both as they were taken to prison and in prison itself.

13. I now ask *all persons who have any concern for truth and justice* the following questions:

1. Is the Toctezinín affair a case of evicting squatters from illegally occupied lands?

2. Do we have a law authorizing the violation of churches or the breaking and entering into private residences, as happened in Chunchi?

3. In this particular instance, should the peasants have followed the instructions they had from IERAC? Instead, should they have yielded to the demands of the lessee and to the threats and other repressive acts with which these demands were supported by the local authorities?

4. Who has violated and scoffed at the provisions of the law—the peasants, IERAC, the Chunchi pastoral team, the lessee, or the provincial authorities of Chimborazo?

5. Is it not shameful and dishonorable for a government that has repeatedly proclaimed its intention to initiate a genuine revolution and to establish justice for the dispossessed then to coun-

tenance the use of methods on the part of its collaborators that demean and crush persons—including physical abuse and murder?

6. By what right has the vicar general of a diocese been thrown into jail and held incommunicado, in flagrant disregard of canon law and accords prevailing between church and state?

Leonidas E. Proaño
Bishop of Riobamba

Riobamba, September 28, 1974

STATEMENT TO THE PRESS BY COLONEL AMERICO ALAVA, GOVERNOR OF RIOBAMBA

Interview published in November 1974 by the Ecuadorian Magazine Vistazo.

Vistazo Magazine: What led to the trouble with Bishop Proaño? What is the official version?

Colonel Americo Alava, Military Governor of Chimborazo: Let me make one thing perfectly clear. At no time, either personally or in my official capacity, did I have any wish whatever to get into an altercation with the bishop of the Diocese of Riobamba, Bishop Proaño. It's not exactly my job to hold Catholic theological disputations. Like a shoemaker, I stick to my own last. My job is law and order, and when law and order are on the line, I have to find a way to reestablish them—always in keeping with the law of the land, of course, and with good and sound principles of justice. This is my only aim. And this is the hardest thing to do—administer justice. Because when you've made your decision, at least one side is going to say you've made the wrong one.

Vistazo: Do you think Bishop Proaño is trying to "start something"? Sow the seeds of dissension, as they say?

Alava: I've never been any good as a mind reader. I don't know what Bishop Proaño is trying to do. I only know what he is actually doing. And so does everybody else in Chimborazo. Everybody can see exactly what he's doing—and his associates better than anybody else.

But I know what I think a priest *ought* to try to do, when he has been promoted to bishop. He ought to try and shepherd his people—keep them on the path of Christian virtue and morality.

Vistazo: But when you jail the vicar general of the diocese, along with a group of peasant organizers—isn't this taking sides with the people who would like to keep an unjust political and social situation going?

Alava: My position is that the law is the same for everybody. The law knows no class distinctions. All must obey it, no matter who they happen to be. And when they break it, they should be punished—again, no matter who they happen to be. Besides, it's the government's job to decide the best way to maintain law and order.

Vistazo: Your Excellency, who do you think would like to see Bishop Proaño out of a job? [An allusion to a petition to the Vatican by a number of civil and religious leaders in Ecuador, demanding Proaño's resignation. The year before, a Vatican investigation had declared Proaño to be "honest and honorable" —Ed.]

Alava: Let me make one thing perfectly clear. We have no investigation under way to determine who would like to see Bishop Proaño out of a job. In the first place, that's for his church superiors to decide. If they think Bishop Proaño should be fired, they can do so. I only know what I read in the papers.

Vistazo: What do you say to all the reports about this that have been made to Rome? And what about the international news wire service that described you as a "fascist"—in a dispatch that was printed right here in Ecuador?

Alava: In the first place, let me say that the international wire services like to distort things—especially when they are written by one of the sides in a dispute. As for calling me a fascist, the one who said that is only showing his complete ignorance of me personally, first of all, and secondly, of what the word itself means philosophically and politically. We all know what "communist" and "fascist" mean in the partisan press—they mean any civil authority with the unmitigated gall to disagree with you.

STATEMENT TO THE PRESS BY
LEONIDAS PROAÑO, BISHOP OF RIOBAMBA

Interview Published in November 1974 by Vistazo.

Vistazo's Borges: Your Excellency, would you justify violence in extreme cases—when there's no other way out?
Bishop Proaño of Riobamba: As Christians we can never be for violence. Our love for our neighbor forbids it. Besides, just from a rational point of view, violence is suicide—the oppressor always has more power than anything a group of peasants can get up.
Vistazo: So you don't agree with Camilo Torres? [Torres was a Colombian priest who was killed as a member of a revolutionary group.]
Proaño: Never for one day of my life have I stopped admiring Camilo Torres—as a priest and as a person. But I think he was wrong. With a faith like that he could have moved mountains. He could have achieved something tremendous. Taking up arms was a mistake. He died before his time, and the church was deprived of an exceptional priest. Take Hélder Câmara, another exceptional priest, who has never favored violence, and we all see what he is doing.
Vistazo: Where do you get all this energy and vigor?
Proaño: From our faith. And from real solidarity. Don't forget: There are only two invincible forces in the twentieth century—the atom bomb, and nonviolence. Don't forget Gandhi, when he gave orders to the untouchables, the pariah masses, to disobey the salt-tax law. Don't forget those soldiers who couldn't pull the trigger.
Vistazo: But they pulled the trigger in Toctezinín.
Proaño: Yes, they did. But maybe for the last time.
Vistazo: What's the idea behind your pastoral teams and your radio schools?

Proaño: Education. Educating the peasants. Fifty-two percent of the population in this province are illiterate. About 90 percent of the peasants are illiterate.

But it's not just material gains we're after. We're trying to apply the documents of Medellín, the bishops' conference, right down to the letter.

We're fighting the Indians' "endemic complexes"—their fatalism, their timidity, their resignation, their servility. And then the other two big things: alcoholism and illiteracy. We've come a long way, but there's still a lot left to do. Don't forget: The Indian has a different mentality from the white. Indians will always follow a leader.

Vistazo: And you're one of the leaders?

Proaño: No. I think of myself as a friend. And I am. The Indians' friend. The idea behind this struggle is to wipe out the exploitation, cruelty, bad treatment, social injustice, repression— all the acts of violence that have been perpetrated on the Indians down through the centuries, in spite of Bartolomé de las Casas. Wipe this out once and for all. [Las Casas was the famous Spanish Dominican in Mexico who fought to protect the Indians from the ravages of Spanish colonialism. His fifth centenary was being celebrated in 1974, the year of this interview.]

Vistazo: When America was discovered, the theologians at Salamanca spent the next ten years debating whether the Indians had souls. They finally decided they did, but that they were "human beings in their minority." In other words, as compared with other human beings, the Indians were children. Do you feel the Indians are still in their minority?

Proaño: Unfortunately, a good many theological conclusions have been dictated by politics. Don't forget: There were saints in favor of the crusades, the Inquisition, and the wars of religion. But to answer your question: All of us are minors when the dominant social group wants it that way.

Our mission is to work for the integral liberation of the Indian—material as well as spiritual. The day the Indians learn to be free, to use their imagination, their creativity—their fantastic creativity—the day we finally manage to help them over their natural lack of self-confidence, Ecuador will be a different place.

Three million Indians in our country! [of a total population of some six million—Ed.]. That's a historical fact that is too important to ignore.

Vistazo: Your plans for your work—your teams, your missionary activity—isn't there a danger? Isn't there a risk of paternalism here?

Proaño: Absolutely. This is why we reflect—why we have periodic evaluations of our pastoral activity.

Vistazo: There's a controversy raging around you. There are people who see signs of radicalism in your actions. They're suspicious of what you're trying to do.

Proaño: We live out on the land, out in the country. We're very naive politically. We have a very, I might say, Manichean mentality—black is black and white is white, and we don't know much about gray. It's the easiest thing in the world to find somebody to call a communist, even when we shout with all our might that Christ, and only Christ, is the Liberator of the human race.

Vistazo: What basic differences are there, do you feel, between Marxism and Christianity?

Proaño: Marxism is fatalistic. Christianity is transcendent. Marxism is interested in getting material rights for people—for many people. Christianity is after the material and spiritual rights of *the human being.* Christianity is moving ahead toward unity, only not by way of totalitarianism—the way the materialist philosophies are. And in any case I've always acted entirely independently. I have no ties whatever with Marxism any more than with the right. There are some mind-sets and some actions that to me seem outmoded, but there's always some bad faith around. In other words I plead for the basic mission of the church ever since it began: denunciation and proclamation. This means denouncing the exploitation of human beings and proclaiming the Good News. I'm a loyal follower of Christ.

Vistazo: In recent years—these years that have been so painful and sorrowful for you—haven't you had any difficulties of faith? I know a number of priests who don't wear their cassocks. I notice you don't wear one either.

Proaño: I've never had a crisis of faith. I've never lost my faith in God. Whenever difficulties come up, they always leave me feeling more faithful to the gospel than before. I have to say, every-thing we've been through these past years has only made me stronger in my faith. Besides, don't forget: Any faith crisis is practically always the dark before the resurrection, before you meet the Lord again.

Vistazo: You had a long meeting with Interior Minister Admiral Poveda, after what happened in Toctezinín. What happened in that meeting? There's been hardly anything about it in the press at all.

Proaño: There was nothing to hide, there is nothing to hide. I laid out the facts, and the minister, who is a sensitive, attentive person, understood the extent of the tragedy. His office had received some "denunciations," making me out to be a guerrilla leader or some kind of technologist of rebellion. There were even some pamphlets distributed saying that our retreat house in Santa Cruz was a kind of dance hall and fun house for "nuns and male religious." You get the tone—"nuns and male religious"—a sneering tone. I think it best not to answer accusations like that. I told the minister essentially that we're people who live by our Christian faith. We work for the poor for purely religious reasons.

Vistazo: Why did you celebrate a Mass on September 11, the anniversary of the fall of President Salvador Allende, the anniversary of his death? Wasn't this just more excuse for people to keep up this campaign against you? Wouldn't you say that was a little rash?

Proaño: I thought it over carefully, then I said I'd celebrate the Mass. The Chileans wanted it for all those who died in Chile. And you know as well as I do—you followed what happened in Chile —hundreds of Catholics, including priests, political militants, peasants, were persecuted, tortured, and murdered during those black days. But these Chileans still had hope, just as we do. So I felt I had to celebrate that Mass—knowing full well the risk I was taking.

Vistazo: You're a leader in the Catholic church. Many people are surprised you go about informally—not "in uniform," so to speak. Why?

Proaño: Bishop's robes always put you at a distance from people. These are critical times—times of anguish and a lack of charity. We have to wipe out the distance between people. There's never been as much need for solidarity and love among persons as there is today. Distance is a sin, every time.

Vistazo: How would you like to die?

Proaño: Surrounded by the peasants, the humble, lowly peasants—and not only by them but by all who see Christ as the sign of genuine liberation.

4.

The Peasants' Battle for Survival

Without a doubt the condition of the peasants in Latin America and in the whole of the Third World is at the heart of the structural changes taking place in world society today. Everywhere rural society is becoming industrialized.

Stupefied, we witness the wholesale eradication of subsistence farming and its replacement by agribusiness for export. Suddenly the law of the jungle rules relationships between small or middle-sized farmers and the great "modern" farms. The conquistadors have withdrawn, and the captains of industry have rushed into the breach.

It is up to the peasantry to transform the law of the jungle into a battle for liberation. Today, it would seem, the true social struggle is no longer the battle of the working classes with the bourgeoisie, but that of Third World peasants seeking to burst the bonds of their domination.

And yet what weapons can Latin American farmers possibly have available to them? The law. And organization. Bully, you will say! Ah, but are not these the twin pillars of all social structure? And if to these two we add a third—resistance—and place it in the very vanguard of the assault—then suddenly the battle against injustice and repression is feasible. Now we have a battle of nonviolence—as hard a combat as any armed one you will ever see. But once the victory is gained, the results will be far more enduring than any pacification by force of arms.

Witness the peasants of the Alagamar estate in Brazil, who won their first battle after three years of dogged struggle.

But the nonviolent combat has its defeats as well. The implacable repression of the Agrarian Leagues of Paraguay is abundant proof of the destructive capacity of brute force.

LETTER TO THE PEASANTS
OF BRAZIL'S ALAGAMAR ESTATE

Pastoral letter on the church's commitment to the weak and oppressed by José Maria Pires, archbishop of João Pessoa, the diocese in which the Alagamar estate is located, and by the auxiliary bishop.

Brothers and Sisters:

One day Jesus went into the Jews' house of prayer and read them this passage from the prophet Isaiah:

> The spirit of the Lord has been given to me,
> for he has anointed me.
> He has sent me to bring the good news to the poor,
> to proclaim liberty to captives,
> and to the blind new sight,
> to set the downtrodden free. . . .
> [Luke 4:18–19; cf. Isa. 61:1].

***

On the occasion of the installation of General Brum Negreiros as commandant of the engineers, General Brum introduced me to General Argus Lima, the commanding general of the Fourth Army. Here is a part of the conversation that took place between us:

General Argus Lima: I'm in the cavalry. You know the cavalry, Your Grace.

Archbishop Pires: I don't know very much about the military,

General. But I should think that if you're in the cavalry you must be like a modern-day knight.

The general: Ever since it was formed, the cavalry has defended the weak—the "orphans and widows," as the Bible calls them.

The archbishop: Then we're working for the same cause, General. The church is more and more on the side of the poor and the oppressed these days.

***

At the recent Archdiocesan Synod, we approved the following directive:

> To maintain solidarity with the people in the defense of their rights, and to denounce whatever constitutes a want of respect for human rights and justice.

And we undertook the following commitment:

> We commit ourselves to living the mystery of the Incarnation more perfectly, by making every effort to be poor with the poor, and thus by abandoning the center of things and making for the edges, the "margins"—without excluding anyone, but always keeping in mind that the gospel is addressed to the poor. We wish to give clear expression to our conviction that it is in the "little ones" of this world that salvation is revealed, and that as their consciousness is raised they become a force for the world's liberation.

***

All three of the statements above—from the gospel, the conversation, and the synodal text—have something in common. They all point to the oppressed, weak, humble people as the center of their interest. All three situations indicate one and the same mission to be embraced by all: The gospel is addressed to the poor; the armed forces should come to the defense of the weak; and the church should be found in the midst of the little ones. It seems appropriate to recall this as we begin Lent this year, when the church in all Brazil is called to pray to the Lord and cry out to men and women: "Work and justice for all!"

The defense of the weak and the battle for the liberation of the oppressed have never been so needful as today. Never as today have the weak been in such danger of being crushed by the machine, by technology, by economic forces. Never as today has the distance been so wide between a mighty minority and the multitude of the weak.

Today the weak one calling out for our protection is no longer just a child crossing a busy street, a hungry orphan, or a widow in need of shelter. Today the weak one in need of protection is the worker trying to eke out a living on the minimum wage, the laborer forced to leave home for other parts, or the small farmer in Alagamar, Piacas, and so many other places being invaded by cattle ranches or sugar cane plantations.

This is the situation on which we wish to reflect in this pastoral letter.

What is Alagamar?

Alagamar is a large estate comprising several villages and plantations, among them Alagamar and Piacas. It is situated in the communes of Itabaiana and Salgado de São Félix.

The former proprietor, Arnaldo Maroja, allowed the peasants to farm the land for their own sustenance and to raise a few head of cattle there. He received his rent on time, and with that he was content. An estimated seven hundred families live on these ten thousand hectars. (The Farmers' Federation counts 446 families or 2,723 persons.)

Mr. Maroja died on November 7, 1975. He had no legal heirs, but left a will providing that these lands should be sold and the revenue distributed to persons named in his will.

Here was a legally unencumbered tract up for sale—a piece of land without an owner. The pastoral workers in the area felt that the federal government ought to buy the ranch, invite a nucleus of settlers there, and set up a shining example of agrarian reform. We feel that the National Institute for Colonization and Agrarian

Reform fell down on the job here, and let slip a wonderful opportunity to apply the Agrarian Reform Statute. The governmental information services were equally remiss in failing to alert the competent authorities of the availability of such a large piece of property.

"For want of a cry, the herd was lost," as they say, and here an extensive tract of unencumbered land fell into the hands of a few individuals, whereas, had the government been informed in time, it could have put this property at the disposition of at least 446 families. Of course there is nothing to prevent the government from resolving the matter in these people's favor even today. It has at its disposal the financial and legal means to do so. It *can* still expropriate the Alagamar property by eminent domain. This is what we wish for with all our heart, and this is what we expect.

The Farmers' Federation has stated:

> Up until the death of Mr. Maroja, the life of these families was calm and peaceful. They could work, raise their crops, and live on the Alagamar estate without being pressurized. Their rights were respected. But now the situation has changed. All this tranquillity has fallen victim to the radical modification of the system at Alagamar. Now we have a regime of unrest, threats, and direct or indirect oppression. Farmers who had worked in serenity now find themselves forced to seek protection and security before they can regain the right to farm their land in peace.[4]

The federation has taken the necessary legal initiatives to protect these farmers, but it admits it can hope for only a short-term solution. According to the federation:

> Only an expropriation of the land for the good of society, in conformity with the provisions of Law 4,504, Article 18, can furnish any definitive solution.
>
> [The federation] is also of the opinion that only the intervention of the competent agencies—INCRA and the Ministry of Agriculture—and the implementation of the Land Statute can offer the farmers any guarantee of continued

residence on the land which they are working and on which their survival depends. Accordingly [the federation] has made application to the president of INCRA, and to the Ministry of Agriculture for a consideration in these terms.[5]

Reactions

What is being done at present by individuals, groups, or organizations at Alagamar? How are the buyers, the farmers, and the federation reacting to the situation?

1. *The buyers:* One of the buyers of a part of the estate has planted sugar cane on fourteen small farms, thereby taking what does not belong to him. Others have created pasture land by fencing off fields on which the farmers have planted their crops. Some of the buyers have brought in cattle and turned them loose to range at will over the people's property, causing damage in the fields and wreaking havoc with the banana crop.

2. *The farmers:* The farmers were united even before the current trouble started. They already shared what they had with one another. When the new crisis arose, they continued to rely on their organizations—the union and the federation. Never have they had recourse to violence. They have made every effort to work within the law, and have sought to enter into negotiations with the authorities. They have dismantled the fences built on their property. They have driven off or fenced in the cattle that were devouring their crops. Some three hundred of them have banded together to pull up the ruinous sugar cane. They have done their best to come to the aid of the eight comrades of theirs who were arrested by order of the authorities or held in custody for reasons of "national security."

3. *The Farmers' Federation:* At first the federation acted with courage and vision, denouncing the acts committed against the farmers and calling for federal expropriation. Then little by little it abandoned the cause—not for want of conviction, but under pressure. Now it functions more as a restraint than an encouragement to the farmers' efforts to remain on their land and to resist the signing of an inequitable agreement.

Our Questions

Who has more right to these lands—the 446 (or 700) families who live here, or a dozen persons living in the lap of luxury in Pernambuco?

Who is the aggressor in the altercation—the buyer who builds fences to make pastures of the farmers' fields, or the farmers who have dismantled the fences?

Which are the aggressors—the buyers who bring in cattle from the outside and turn them loose in the fields, or the farmers who drive off the cattle or fence them in to keep them from ravaging their crops?

Which is the aggressor—the buyer who plants sugar cane on another's property, or those who uproot the cane to protect what is theirs?

Who is the aggressor—the peaceful resident of thirty, forty, fifty years or more, or newcomers who, simply because they have more money, arrogate to themselves absolute proprietorship of the land?

If the aggression is on the part of the new owners, why have only farmers so far been arrested or jailed when their only act is the defense of their rights by nonviolent means?

Our Reasoning

The church of La Paraiba has taken a stand. It is on the side of the farmers of Alagamar. It does so out of fidelity to the gospel and love for the people. Like Jesus Christ, some of us have made our option for the oppressed. We are all too aware that we are as yet far from having made this commitment to the hilt. But we are heading in the right direction, and the number of us who have made a commitment to the people is on the increase. We are not against the rich, any more than Jesus Christ is against the rich. But we are against the ambition of certain rich persons who throw up obstacles to the development of the poor.

The primary criterion of a nation's development is not the industries it possesses or its exports or its income. The primary criterion of development is the welfare of its population. In a well-organized society the means of production should be placed at the service of the common good, and not of the accumulation of wealth by individuals. The buyers of Alagamar have no need of these lands in order to live. By contrast, the farmers who live and work there depend on the lands for their survival. The common good therefore demands these lands' expropriation.

We declare that sheer purchase can never be the sole, or even the principal, basis of property rights. Both need and toil are nobler and more legitimate titles. The one who has need of the land has more right to it than the one who does not; and the one who has lovingly worked that land for his or her own sustenance is more its possessor than one who has abundant wealth, yes, but who has "never sowed a solitary seed."

It is said that our law recognizes only the proprietorship of one who has made a purchase—that he or she alone may have legal title. But must we not recognize that what is legal is not always legitimate or more legitimate? The farmers and their organizations have been waging a campaign for the legalization of the right that springs from need and toil. The government recognized that right at Mucatu, a smaller estate with fewer families; it can do so all the more at Alagamar and like cases until such time as new legislation confirms the right of the weak and needy. Indeed, in a certain manner, we already have this legislation in the form of the Land Statute, which has just such cases as Alagamar in mind:

> Expropriation by public authority in priority zones shall take place . . . in regions having a large number of farmers, tenant farmers, and property holders [Article 20, v].

Under these terms the Alagamar property eminently qualifies. It is located in a zone classified in the Agrarian Reform as "having priority." It supports hundreds of tenant farmers and property holders.

Brazil, as we know, has the capability of putting an end to the poverty of the people of the countryside. Of course, this requires a new orientation in farm policy—one that assigns priority to the production of foodstuffs for home comsumption and not of manufactured goods for export. But this new orientation ill suits the interests of the mighty; hence it is an orientation that will not be taken until the people finally move to make our nation aware of how much they suffer. This is the way it was with God's people in exile in Egypt. And it was ever thus, all down through history.

Today the church is helping the people organize, helping them take responsibility for their advancement, and helping them seek the transformation of structures of oppression and the reform of laws that prevent them from substantially improving their living conditions.

The church believes that the attitude of three hundred small farmers united to defend the property of a few comrades is evidence of the people's great maturity. This attitude deserves the respect and applause of all in favor of national development. And it deserves the particular respect and applause of those who bear direct responsibility for order and security. Here is a perfect example of order. And the laborers themselves provide for the security of all concerned.

The Farmers' Federation especially can be proud of the rich harvest it has reaped in the battle to raise the farm laborers' class consciousness. The federation must not allow such a vigorous and promising crop to run to weeds or to be pulled up by the roots.

We therefore denounce as a grave miscarriage of responsibility the demand, issued on the fifteenth of last month to the president of the federation and one of its attorneys, that the federation urge the farmers who have been arrested to agree to the accord and abandon the struggle for their rights. This means in the case of the Alagamar property abandoning the demand for the implementation of Law 4,504 of November 30, 1964. We denounce maneuvers of every sort—intimidation, threats, insinuations, and promises—that are calculated to deprive the farmers of their solid right to demand exclusive proprietorship of this land.

Conclusion

We do not believe that we are alone in taking this stand in favor of small farmers victimized by pressure and injustice. Our story is familiar all over this land.

These are Indians driven from their reservations. These are

shanty dwellers who have been wiped out by urbanization. These are small farmers brought to their knees by agribusiness. We know the road will be long and dolorous. So was the journey of God's people in the desert. But the victory is sure, for God has made himself the mighty Ally of the little ones and has promised them the kingdom.

We hereby serve notice on all who glory in the name of Christian and profess faith in the Catholic church: we remind them that God's plan is contemned when apt conditions for development are denied human groups like those of Alagamar. For "God's glory is a human being fully alive."[6]

We invite all who have perceived the justice of this cause to join their voices with ours for the defense of the weak and oppressed. We suggest that they send telegrams to the authorities, recalling how urgent it is to accede to the request of the Farmworkers' Federation of the state of La Paraiba for the expropriation of the Alagamar estate.

We propose to farmers everywhere that they write to their brothers and sisters of Alagamar words of encouragement and support. They may send their letters care of the Archbishop's Residence, P. O. Box 13, 58.000 João Pessoa, Paraiba, and we shall forward them.

We ask everyone to send a copy of all correspondence addressed to the authorities, the peasant organizations, or the Alagamar farmers to the Center for the Defense of Human Rights at the same address at the Archbishop's Residence. These letters will be included in the center's dossier on Alagamar. We ask our parishes, religious houses, basic Christian communities, and meditation groups to do the same. We also ask them to include the intention of our sisters and brothers of Alagamar among their petitions in the Prayer of the Faithful.

We shall gratefully receive any contribution that other persons or institutions might wish to make lest the farmers weaken in the struggle for want of material means.

Finally, in order the more completely to share in the Passion of Christ that is present in the sufferings of our brothers and sisters of farm, factory, and fishery—Indians and whites alike—I invite those Christians who are able to do so to join me in a day of fasting and prayer that God may rise up and work the liberation of his people. Let us offer this day on Friday, March 17, the Feast of the Seven Sorrows of Our Blessed Lady.

This pastoral letter is to be read to the faithful at the next Sunday Mass and at the next meeting of each basic community and meditation group. Let it also be filed in the archives.*

João Pessoa
February 12, 1978
The First Sunday of Lent

José Maria Pires
Archbishop of La Paraiba

Marcelo Carvalheiro
Auxiliary Bishop

PARAGUAY: THE INCIDENT AT JEJUÍ

Declaration by the Ecclesiastical Authorities of Concepción.

San Isidro Surrounded and Dispersed

1. Some 300 kilometers from Asunción and 250 kilometers from Concepción at the intersection of Routes 3 and 5 stands the farming colony called San Isidro de Jejuí, in Lima Parish of the Department of San Pedro.

This settlement is composed of some two dozen families, a Catholic priest, a community of male contemplatives (the Little Brothers of Jesus), and some members of the Association of Secular Missioners from Spain.

The members of this settlement, under the supervision of the local hierarchy, undertook an experiment in community living ac-

---

*On November 9, 1978, the Federal Government of Brazil partially acceded to the demands of the peasants of Alagamar and decreed the expropriation of a first tract of 2,000 hectars.—Ed.

cording to the gospel, especially as described in Acts 2:42 and 4:32 and in the spirit of Vatican II and Medellín.

This interesting experiment in Christian renewal spread to other localities in the Diocese of Concepción as well.

2. On February 8, 1975, at daybreak, a detail of some seventy soldiers under the command of Lt. Col. José Félix Grau invaded the settlement of San Isidro de Jejuí. They surprised the residents in their sleep since it was about four o'clock in the morning.

3. Coincidentally present in the community at the time were Monsignor Roland Bordelon, regional director for South America of Catholic Relief Service and Kevin A. Kalahan, director of the Paraguayan Program of Catholic Relief Service, both citizens of the United States.

4. As the above-mentioned Americans looked on, Father Braulio Maciel panicked near the house of the Little Brothers of Jesus, who were French nationals. While attempting to flee to safety, Maciel was felled by a bullet in the leg from a .38 caliber revolver. Thereupon he was carried to a waiting van and driven to San Estanislao, where he received first aid. Then he was taken to Buenos Aires.

As Father Maciel lay stretched out on the ground, some peasants attempted to approach him to protect him from further harm. But when they were given the command "Hit the dirt!" they quickly fell to the ground. In this supine position they were beaten with clubs.

5. In the course of this operation, all the inhabitants' dwellings were entered and searched. Among the items ransacked were books, Bibles, notes, and minutes of the peasants' Christian meditation groups. According to our information, there also disappeared a sum of money in the amount of 900,000 guaranis, which had been donated by Catholic organizations in Europe for the purchase of several hectars of land. Another sum on the order of 100,000 guaranis was also missing. It was intended to defray the costs of the forthcoming meeting at Asunción of the Little Brothers with their superior general from Rome. Both of these sums had been entrusted to the Little Brothers of Jesus for safekeeping.

6. The following persons were arrested in the course of the mili-

tary operation and taken to the offices of the Central Bureau of Investigation in the capital:

—Monsignor Roland Bordelon and Kevin Kalahan were held incommunicado for forty-eight hours and prevented from con-tacting either each other or the ambassador of their country.

—Brothers Juan Penard and Juan Trembais, both of French nationality, were bound to one another by a length of cord.

—Ms. Del Pilar Larraya, a member of the Secular Missioners.

—The following Paraguayans: the Reverend Braulio Maciel, who was wounded by a bullet; he is a priest of the Diocese of Concepción assigned to the farming colony and a member of the Paraguayan Episcopal Conference's Commission for Social Pastoral Works; Mr. Carlos Cabrera, one of a group preparing for ordination as permanent deacons and a member of the National Council for the Permanent Diaconate; Messrs. Apolonio Alvarez, Antonio Vera, Spiridión Martínez, and Cleto Benítez, and Ms. Modesta Ferreira.

On the following day—Sunday, February 9—Father Neil Rodriguez, a native of Trinidad and Tobago and a member of the Congregation of the Fathers of the Holy Ghost, celebrated the Eucharist at the colony of San Roque on the banks of the River Jejuí. After Mass he was arrested and taken to the capital.

To date it has been impossible to obtain reliable information concerning the persons and goods seized during the military assault on the colony of San Isidro or concerning the persons held at the Central Bureau of Investigation.

7. On Monday, February 10, Bishop Aníbal Maricevich of Concepción came to San Isidro at 10:30 a.m. and tried to enter the community that had been so cruelly surprised by the action of the troops. He was accompanied by two priests and a Marist Brother. No sooner did Bishop Maricevich attempt to carry out his pastoral duties by showing charity to the suffering families of the community than he was categorically refused entry into the area by the commander of the military task force.

At this point the bishop and the military commander engaged in a long discussion of a number of points concerning the peasant movement in the light of the general teaching of the church as well as the motives for the military intervention.

Lt. Col. José F. Grau stated, among other things, that he had read a large part of the confiscated written material and that their content corresponded to the explanations offered by His Excellency, the bishop of the diocese. We declare that at no time did Lt. Col. Grau claim to have found arms, subversive literature, material for the training of guerrilla activists, or the like. During the discussion an aircraft repeatedly flew over the area, doubtless for the purpose of reconnaissance.

8. The peasant community of San Isidro—men, women, and children—is totally cut off from the outside world. The insecurity and suffering of its residents are really acute. For all we know, some basic food supplies may already be lacking. We do not know whether the peasants may be in need of a physician. But we have to add that, with all their confusion and perplexity, these people are maintaining an attitude of serenity and generosity, living the mystery of the cross and the joy of witnessing to the gospel.

9. *Measures taken:*

a) At eleven o'clock in the morning of February 11, Bishop Aníbal Maricevich of Concepción sought an audience with Minister of the Interior Dr. Sabino Augusto Montanaro; the request was refused.

b) The Permanent Council of the Paraguayan Bishops' Conference received a report on the events described above; it decided on certain steps that should be taken.

c) Faced with the impossibility of meeting with the civil authorities, the bishop of Concepción turned to the military vicar, Bishop Juan Moleón Andreu, in the latter's capacity as liaison person between church and state. The vicar addressed a memorandum to the civil authorities containing the following requests: *(i)* Authorization to visit and assist those held by the Central Bureau of Investigation, especially Father Maciel, who had been wounded; *(ii)* Authorization for unrestricted communication with the members of the San Isidro community for the purpose of bearing them the help they need and deserve.

d) The embassies of the United States, France, Spain, and the United Kingdom were informed of the arrest of their respective nationals.

10. In spite of all these efforts, the arrests go on: (1) on February 12, Messrs. Evangelista Nuñez, Oscar Cardozo, and the latter's eldest son, Victorino Cardozo, were detained. Nuñez and the

elder Cardozo are enrolled in a program for preparation for the diaconate on behalf of the parish of San Estanislao; (2) on February 13, the Reverend Dante Frattani, an Italian national and a member of the Third Order of Saint Francis, was arrested. He is the pastor of the parish of San Estanislao; (3) in the nation's capital Messrs. Mauricio Alcaraz and Juan M. Escobar were arrested.

Under these conditions, the fears and anxiety of Christian organizations in the Diocese of Concepción are understandable, for their members are under constant threat. There are all the indications of an intention to dissolve the colony of San Isidro de Jejuí and disperse its families.*

Concepción,
February 15, 1975

ANNOUNCEMENT BY THE SERVICE FOR NONVIOLENT ACTION IN LATIN AMERICA

The situation is serious for the peasants of the Christian communities of Jejuí, Acaray, Yvyruga, and Caaguazu, and for the parish school in Tuna Santa Rosa. The people there are being victimized—subjected to repression, imprisoned, and tortured—as a result of government accusations that their communities are "hotbeds of subversion." The allegations are false and groundless, as even the armed forces and police have been able to verify. And yet the persecution continues:

1. The Commune of San Isidro de Jejuí remains cordoned off by soldiers and police. Its residents are continuously insulted, threatened, and harrassed by rifle and machine-gun fire. They are completely cut off from contact with the outside. Prevented from harvesting their crops, they are pressured to leave their settlement by reports that the land has been bought by some Brazilians.

2. So far the people have sufficient food supplies. But they are prohibited from purchasing anything whatsoever. They are in

*According to subsequent reports, peasants have been murdered in the region. —Ed.

need of medical attention, especially the women and children.

3. The chapel has been desecrated. The sacred vessels were removed by the police, and the consecrated hosts had to be retrieved from the floor by the peasants and religious.

4. The bishop of the Diocese of Concepción, Aníbal Maricevich, is forbidden to enter the enclosure. According to official sources, the bishop will not be allowed into the compound until the community has been dispersed.

5. Ecclesiastical authorities are prohibited from visiting the religious and peasants held in jail. Some of these persons are in delicate condition and in need of better medical attention.

6. Father Braulio Maciel, who was wounded by a soldier's bullet, is still in custody. Held incommunicado in a hospital, he is allowed only occasional visits from his aged father, under strict surveillance. Maciel is forbidden all contact with church authorities.

7. Some sixty-five peasants and religious are currently in prison at the Central Bureau of Investigation and in the Federal Penitentiary.

8. On March 10 another religious was escorted to the Argentine border and expelled from Paraguay at the Clarinda checkpoint. He is Father Erwin J. Kohmann, a Franciscan who had been exercising his pastoral ministry in the community of Acaray. His arrest and expulsion were effectuated without valid reason or any explanation whatever.

9. On Sunday, March 16, a letter of His Excellency, Archbishop Rolón of Asunción, was read in all the churches of the archdiocese. The archbishop denounced the torture and repression to which Christian communities and the people in general have fallen victim. He asked the prayers of all the faithful for peace and a just reconciliation.

10. The Reverend Norbert Bellini* denies having made the statement attributed to him in a France-Presse dispatch appearing in the Buenos Aires daily *La Razón:*

*Father Bellini is an Italian priest working in the Paraguayan countryside. A member of the International Fellowship of Reconciliation, he represented the nonviolent movement at meetings of the Second Russell Tribunal that dealt with repression in Latin America. These meetings were held in Europe between 1973 and 1976.

Rome, Feb. 27 (ANSA)—"I categorically deny the report published on January 17 of this year by a Buenos Aires newspaper, quoting a dispatch carried by an international wire service, to the effect that I have made inflammatory statements concerning an approaching armed struggle to be waged by the people of Paraguay," said Italian priest Norberto Bellini, a missionary in Paraguay who is involved with the peasant movement there. Bellini, currently visiting Italy, added: "The International Fellowship of Nonviolence demands that the agency that circulated the false report produce its evidence." The priest, who had reported on the social and economic situation in Paraguay to the Second Russell Tribunal in Brussels, handed reporters copies of editorials appearing in the Paraguayan press that attacked the alleged statements. He added that he had been the victim of a "violent attack" on a Paraguayan National Radio all-network broadcast. Bellini stated that the Second Russell Tribunal had sent to Rome a tape recording of his address and the following discussion. He said that the tape, which had been played publicly, proved that the statements attributed to him by the wire service were, in fact, not made. The Second Russell Tribunal, for its own part, announced the "permanent availability of the recording to the authorities on demand." Finally, Bellini put speculation regarding his Brussels address to rest by citing the French daily *Le Monde* [for December 5, 1974] to the effect that no statement like that attributed to Bellini had been made. Instead, the priest had spoken of a "liberation action inspired by active nonviolence."

11. The intervention of the International Red Cross as well as that of other organizations has been sought in order to verify the facts of the situation and to persuade the government of Paraguay to lift the blockade of the communities in question. This would permit the reestablishment of contact with the outside, especially for the purpose of furnishing medical attention and establishing communications with church authorities. It would also permit an investigation into the situation and condition of those

who have been jailed, and afford an opportunity to supply them with any medical care that may be required.

Buenos Aires, March 24, 1975
Adolfo Pérez Esquivel,
Coordinator General for Latin America

THE BELLINI AFFAIR: A CONTROVERSY OVER THE NONVIOLENCE OF THE AGRARIAN LEAGUES

Letter of the Reverend Norberto Bellini to Sendero, *the official weekly publication of the Paraguayan Bishops' Conference, concerning the government of Paraguay's accusation that Father Bellini was fomenting subversion. The letter was published in the March 21, 1975, issue of* Sendero.

Brussels, Belgium
February 18, 1975

To the Publisher of *Sendero*
Paraguayan Bishop's Conference
Asunción, Paraguay

Sir:

This letter is for publication in *Sendero*. Only this morning I learned of a series of accusations lodged against a certain "Armando Bellini," who is said to have appeared as a "witness" at the Second Session of the Russell Tribunal in Brussels. It is alleged that this person made a number of declarations concerning supposed ties between the People's Revolutionary Army of Argentina and the Agrarian Leagues of Paraguay.[7]

In view of the public character of these allegations, I wish to make an open declaration before the public opinion of Paraguay.

Although the name is not mine, I nevertheless suppose it is I who am meant, since the last name is the same as mine and since I was indeed at attendance at the Second Session of the Russell Tribunal. I was not there, however, as a "witness," but as an expert, a *relator,* or *rapporteur.* (There is a great deal of difference, from the juridical point of view, between a witness, whether for the prosecution or for the defense, and an expert summoned to testify in the area of his or her particular specialization.)

1. My testimony, in my capacity as an expert, was both recorded and published. This oral and written documentation is available to anyone who may wish to hear or read it. I am having a copy of my testimony sent to you today under separate cover. Further copies may be obtained from the Permanent Secretariat of the Tribunal by writing the presiding justice: Senator Lelio Basso, President of the Second Session of the Russell Tribunal, Senate of the Republic, Rome, Italy. You may also write the vice-president of the tribunal: Dr. François Rigaux, professor of international law, The Catholic University of Louvain, Belgium.

It will be a matter of no difficulty for the Paraguayan authorities to obtain this tape and/or transcript through their embassies in Belgium or Italy.

2. I delivered my report in the Great Hall of the *Palais des Congrès* in Brussels, where the Second Session of the International Russell Tribunal II had convened to an audience of a thousand people, including journalists from all over the world. These journalists could be called, if need be, to attest to the content of my statements. Furthermore, a program of the proceedings, listing the names and addresses of all the participants (justices, members of the jury and press, observers, experts, and witnesses), was prepared for the purpose of verifying the identity of all who entered the hall. This program is also available from the same permanent secretariat in Rome.

3. In this second session the tribunal did not undertake to analyze the political implications of matters under consideration, as would be implied by the declarations attributed to me. Instead, it only considered the economic mechanisms of internal and external dependency in Latin America—that is, the problem of national monopolies and multinational corporations.

My report, as can be gathered from my recorded and published text, did indeed concern Paraguay. In fact *it was based on docu-*

ments and statistics published in Paraguay itself, of which I am prepared to furnish an ample dossier if this is necessary.

4. At no time did I speak "in the name of, and as representing, the Agrarian Leagues of Paraguay." I spoke only and solely in my own behalf as a veteran of eleven years with the Paraguayan peasants in my efforts to contribute something to their integral development. Working at the grassroots, I, of course, worked in concert with teams of the Agrarian Leagues of Misiones Province.

5. In view of the accusations against me issuing from Paraguay, the International Fellowship of Reconciliation, of which I am an international secretary, the War Resisters International, and several other international movements, will now initiate a world-wide campaign of information and clarification. In addition, these groups will undertake the necessary legal steps with their respective governments in numerous countries on all continents to bring my emphatic and categorical disavowal of these groundless allegations to the attention of the public in the international press.

(Rev.) Norberto Bellini
International Secretary,
International Fellowship of Reconciliation

CHURCH AUTHORITIES TAKE A STAND

Statement of the Paraguayan Bishops' Conference and the Federation of Religious of Paraguay Concerning Recent Incidents in That Country.

March 8, 1975

In view of recent events of a very serious nature, reported throughout the country in a distorted form, the Paraguayan Bishops' Conference and the Federation of Religious of Paraguay, gathered in extraordinary session, deem themselves under the obligation to make the following statements:

1. The church, profoundly identifying with the soul and longings of the people of Paraguay, has ever sought the good of this land, as the whole course of our national history abundantly attests, especially at those critical moments in that history when the creation and growth of our nation were most in jeopardy.

2. In recent years a great number of incidents have occasioned the deterioration of our national community. The church therefore, at the urgent appeal of the Roman pontiff, has celebrated the Holy Year of Jubilee as a Year of National Reconciliation, calling upon all sectors of our society to seek after a genuine unity based on truth and justice. In this way the church has not only supported the appeal of the President of the Republic for a "national dialogue," but has gone even further, furnishing this dialogue with an inner spirit.

3. To the rising sorrow and concern of all sincere citizens of Paraguay, especially of ourselves as responsible for the religious welfare of the faithful, there have occurred in recent months a series of incidents of a particularly grave and serious nature. These events have been reported to the public with groundless ideological interpretations.

Such incidents are the occasion of anxiety, insecurity, and suffering at every level of society. A great number of Christians, including members of religious orders and communities and institutions under church direction, have been the victims of various forms of violence.

A tendentious propaganda seeks to sow discord and mistrust of the hierarchy among God's people. But in broad sectors of the Paraguayan people it provokes revulsion for and animosity toward its authors instead.

4. The common element in all the aforesaid incidents is the allegation accompanying them—usually by radio, newspapers, or addresses delivered at political meetings and rallies, or even in ministerial communiqués, and in every instance without evidence —of a "Marxist orientation" or "ties with ideological organizations devoted to subversive activity." Such orientations and ties would be at odds with the teaching of the church. As a result, if such claims were true, they would be rejected energetically by the legitimate ecclesiastical authorities in our country.

5. Furthermore, the conduct of the persons charged with the

implementation of these repressive measures has in most cases been violent and arbitrary; it has been in flagrant violation of the national constitution as well as of human rights and dignity. The incidents touching ecclesiastical persons or institutions have been characterized by a neglect or contempt for legitimate ecclesiastical authority as well.

It is especially painful to us to consider how lamentable an image of Paraguay is being projected before the eyes of democratic nations by this manner of proceeding. For in a number of cases the victims of these arbitrary actions have been not only Paraguayan nationals but also citizens of other nations who had been attempting to serve the church and the people of our land.

6. National public opinion is aware, however inadequately, of incidents that have taken place at Numi, Eugenio A. Garay, Cordillera, Jejuí, and other localities of the Second Department as well as more recently at Santa Rosa Misiones. It is also aware of the insidious campaigns conducted against the hierarchy, the Catholic University, and other institutions and social works of the church, and of the systematic distortion of fact upon which these propaganda campaigns are based.

Questions Arise

These incidents and events are altogether inexplicable in view of the fact that they are instigated by two groups: *(a)* A political party—the Republican National Association—which, on more than one occasion in its long history and under the leadership of some of its most illustrious scions, has proudly flown the banner of the struggle for authentic Christian values; and *(b)* elements of an army which, in its glorious and heroic deeds in war as in peace, has ever sought the endorsement and support of the Christian fortress, the church.

In view of this development, we, the bishops of Paraguay and the major religious superiors, now raise the following questions:

1. How does it happen that certain elements in a party and an army comprised mainly of Catholics can behave like regimes that persecute the church?

Surely the government of a Catholic country has at its disposal other avenues of approach. Such a government will respect the institutional church and make an effort to grasp the import of its mission with all the pastoral and social engagements such a mission implies. For the resolution of differences with the church it will use the possibilities of dialogue with the legitimate pastors of that church.

2. How should we interpret the astounding rage and fury of this persecution—altogether disproportionate and cruel from every viewpoint—of the church's efforts at evangelization and development? After all, such efforts are being carried on in behalf of the poorest citizens of our nation, most of whom are themselves members of the Colorado party.

3. What justification can we find for a systematic, unremitting anti-Christian campaign conducted by the official organs of that party—*Patria* and *La Voz de Coloradismo*—without implicating those guilty of this persecution in the pollution of the very ideals of their own Republican National party and the betrayal of the heritage of so many of its illustrious figures?

4. We call particular attention to the repeated allegation of "Marxist infiltration" in the church. Doubtless this claim has been made with a view to sowing doubt and fear among the rank and file of the party as well as among the people of the nation at large. Are the civil and military authorities aware of the origin of this allegation or of the ulterior motives of those who seek to spread it?

The Church Takes a Stand

There is no doubt that the seriousness of these incidents is a matter of great concern to the bishops and major religious superiors of Paraguay. These occurrences seem to have been provoked for the express purpose of instilling in a people who have rallied to the ideals of one of our nation's most important political parties an attitude of betrayal of the most basic principles of that party's political philosophy, as well as a denial of its dearest historical traditions. As the legitimate pastors of the church, we further denounce these incidents and campaigns as anti-Christian and contrary to the values of the gospel.

In these circumstances and in the light of the questions we have raised, the Paraguayan Bishops' Conference and the Federation of Religious of Paraguay feel themselves obliged to make the following statements:

1. Out of fidelity to the gospel and solicitude for the common welfare of Paraguay, the church maintains, and will continue to maintain at every moment, its commitment to the defense and promotion of the basic human rights recognized by our country's constitution. At the same time the church will continue to be with all its might the voice of men and women who have no voice to raise in their own defense.

2. The church intends to maintain the legitimate independence and liberty belonging to it by divine right—in its being, in its task, and in the life of its institutions.

3. The church calls attention to the proper Christian respect it shows to the civil authorities. It points out the constancy of its commitment to collaborate with those authorities in all tasks that promote the common good.

A Call to Christians

In conclusion, we hereby issue an appeal to the whole people of God to maintain and deepen a genuinely Christian attitude in the face of the above-cited lamentable incidents:

1. We beg the victims of violence to live in the faith, hope, and love of Christ. Know that your fellow Christians stand ready to support and aid you. This is especially true of ourselves, the shepherds of the people of God.

2. We beg the authors and instigators of the above-cited incidents to reexamine their intentions, attitudes, and decisions in a spirit of penitence in order that, in all truth and justice, they may be able to stand with unsullied consciences before the judgment seat of God, who will render judgment on human beings and their history.

3. We beg the authorities responsible for the above-cited situations to make haste to free the imprisoned and to repair the harm that has been wrought.

4. We beg all who observe the course of these events not to allow themselves to be swayed by tendentious propaganda and unjust accusations.

5. We beg all Christians everywhere to unite their efforts for

the promotion of an authentic community of sisters and brothers among all the citizens of our country through their fidelity to the gospel and the church, as is fitting for the people of God.

Penitential Celebration

In token of the conversion of souls and the earnest commitment of the church, we ask all Christians to participate in the penitential services that will be celebrated in all the churches of our country on this coming Sunday, March 18, 1975. The purpose of all Christians should be to offer to God, in union with their pastors, a true prayer of brothers and sisters. Let us offer our prayer for the victims of this persecution and for the conversion of the persecutors. Let us also pray that the church will be loyal to its mission to evangelize and defend human beings and their dignity.

The Paraguayan Bishops' Conference

The Federation of Religious of Paraguay

Appendix A

Latin America's Charter of Nonviolence

Evangelical nonviolence is a mighty force for liberation. Such is the simple statement being made today by some Christians of Latin America. Such is their response to the violence—both structural and circumstantial—that scars the life of their region.

There is something called gospel radicalism.

But it is not the perverted radicalism that ends up in totalitarianism— the unhealthy fruit of an alliance between religious dogmatism and political despotism. From the Europe of the Inquisition to the Iran of the ayatollahs, alas, is not a very long or difficult road.

Gospel radicalism is a radicalism that prevents us from growing accustomed to evil. It keeps us from lapsing into the "silence of the good" of which Adolfo Pérez Esquivel spoke in the early pages of this book. Gospel radicalism is a radicalism that stakes the absolutely basic claim to dignity of the poor of the earth. It is the one that gives us the courage to stand up to Caesar and remind him of God's command—God whose Face flashes forth in the visage of the humble and the lowly.

The Christians of Latin America joyfully remind us that the combat for justice is not a monopoly of Leninist Marxism. Surely Christians hold no magical key to social organization, any more than anyone. But they are in possession of a rich wellspring of power for liberation that surges up out of the deep awareness within the human heart.

The message of these Christians deserves a hearing.

DECLARATION OF THE INTERNATIONAL MEETING OF LATIN AMERICAN BISHOPS ON "NONVIOLENCE: A POWER FOR LIBERATION," NOVEMBER 28–DECEMBER 3, 1977

Rarely does one have the opportunity to experience such a friendly, simple, and warm encounter. Our meeting brought together twenty bishops, some priests, and some members of the laity from nine Latin American countries—Brazil, Bolivia, Peru, Venezuela, Nicaragua, El Salvador, Chile, Ecuador, and Panama. We have enjoyed a most rich experience of fellowship and community here in Bogotá.

We were invited here by the International Movement for Reconciliation, Pax Christi, the Latin American Caritas Secretariat, and the Peace and Justice Service, an organization dedicated to nonviolence. Our inaugural session was presided over by His Eminence, Aloisio Cardinal Lorscheider, and the theme of our reflection was the situation of violence in Latin America—together with the Christian response of nonviolence as a social force and as the liberating answer provided in the gospel itself. We determined that this would be our way of expressing our deep communion with the Holy Father, who had selected as the theme for the World Day of Peace in 1978: "No to violence, yes to peace."

We came from many lands. And we came bearing with us the witness of a church that is committed to the very poorest, including those for whom poverty means the sacrifice of the gift of life itself. We came bearing tidings of the mighty deeds of many in our lands who state their witness to Christian love by pouring out their blood for justice, for peace, and for the defense of the weak and oppressed.

From the moment we began our deliberations, it seemed to us that if our closing statement was not sealed in our own blood and our own sacrifice, it would fail to have any deep meaning: It would not point to the radicalism of the gospel. Indeed, we felt the finest moments of our gathering here were our times of prayer and celebration. For we took the text of Isaiah 53 and used it to try to identify and recognize the suffering servants who are today's incarnation of the mystery of the Lord and of his work of redemption.

Altogether aware that we, too, are sinners and responsible—together with our brothers and sisters—for injustice in the world, we fasted from all food and drink for twenty-four hours on December 1 as an act of penance and as a small token of our communion with the half billion hungry of the world. The world's hungry are impatient for the world to become a just place where all men and women will at last be regarded as children of the same Father. It was in this atmosphere that we have prepared this declaration.

We are concerned about the situation of violence that so deeply scars the life and history of our peoples. Sorrowfully we note that "the scandal of the glaring inequalities, not merely in the enjoyment of possessions but even more in the exercise of power'' (*Populorum Progressio* 9) is actually increasing. The situation of sin we denounced at our conference in Medellín has continued unabated, if indeed it has not actually deteriorated.

We live in a whole climate of violence. There is violence in the area of economics by reason of acute fiscal crises, the repeated devaluation of our currencies, unemployment, and soaring taxes—the burden of which ultimately falls on the poor and helpless. There is violence at the political level, as our people in varying degrees are deprived of their right of self-expression and self-determination and of the exercise of their civil rights. Still more grave in many countries are human-rights violations in the form of torture, kidnappings, and murder. Violence also makes its appearance in various forms of delinquency, in drug abuse as an escape from reality, in the mistreatment of women—all tragic expressions of frustration and of the spiritual and cultural decadence of a people losing their hope in tomorrow.

Here we may not scurry for cover to empty theories or hide behind condemnations of one group by another group. The violence is here; it is a fact. Injustice exists; this is reality. As Christians we may not abide this. We may not allow ourselves to grow accustomed to evil, least of all to an evil that is daily and constant. We may not keep silent, especially when people try to intimidate us with threats, campaigns of vilification, and reprisals. And still less may we brook the presentation of violence as an exigency of the faith—for the defense of "humanistic, Christian values."

Hence, very simply we now seek to present the fruit of our reflections to the ecclesial communities of Latin America. First we shall lay out the facts as we see them. Then we shall plead for an energetic, radical, but evangelical solution, springing from the teaching and example of the Lord Jesus, whom we proclaim as the true and sole Lord of history. For the gospel is the mighty incarnation not only of God's truth but also of his power, a power at work in history in order to transform it. We believe in the fecundity of action inspired by love, as His Holiness Pope Paul VI has preached so many times. We prefer this action to any violence. Violence is un-Christian and unevangelical, not to mention inefficacious.

Violence in Latin America

If we undertake to speak here of violence in Latin America, it is without the least desire to suggest that violence is missing anywhere on the face of our globe. Nor in stressing the evils of violence, are we for a moment denying signs of hope for the future. Only these signs are not primarily to be found in political or economic "gains," such as in the stability that may be afforded by authoritarian regimes or the improvement of certain sectors of the economy. No, gains of this ilk often camouflage a heavy price that is paid by the marginalized masses in terms of violence wrought upon their persons. The real signs of hope are rather in the raised consciousness of the people, in the solidarity of a community of sisters and brothers, in mutual assistance, and in the search for a more just and humane society. For it is here that we see the liberating activity of the Holy Spirit. Here are the true "goods," which:

> . . . we will find . . . again, but freed of stain, burnished and trans-figured. . . . This will be so when Christ hands over to the Father a kingdom eternal and universal: "a kingdom of truth and life, of holiness and grace, of justice, love, and peace" [*Gaudium et Spes* 39].

Violence in the Economic Domain

We hereby draw attention to and denounce the violence that prevails in the international marketplace of manufactured goods and raw materials. We declare with Paul VI:

> . . . social justice requires that it restore to the participants a certain equality of opportunity. This equality is a long-term objective, but to reach it, we must begin now to create true equality in discussions and negotiations [*Populorum Progressio* 61].

However the poor nations may struggle to make their voices heard and have their claims admitted, international conferences make no progress. Solutions are postponed until now they have become a matter of the most urgent necessity. The people's just longings for a new economic order fail to find translation into concrete measures calculated to restore hope to the poor of Latin America.

The international situation also has repercussions on the internal options a country may make. The development models selected reduce the quality of life of the masses of the people; and any reforms that have already been undertaken, such as the agrarian reform, seem to be obliged to come to a halt or even, in certain countries, actually to regress.

By contrast, the power of the large industrial conglomerates, whose outlays have been known to dwarf the budgets of whole Latin American nations, enjoys uncontrolled expansion, both in scope and in degree. The benefits accruing from hosting these transnational enterprises with the capital and technology they bring to our lands does not appear to compensate for the risks we run at their hands, for their power is one which enables them to:

> carry out autonomous strategies which are largely independent of the national political powers and therefore not subject to control from the point of view of the common good. By extending these activities, these private organizations can lead to a new form of economic domination on the social, cultural, and even political level [*Octogesima Adveniens* 44].

And hereby the whole Latin American integration effort lies in ruins. Other practitioners of economic violence are persons who send their wealth abroad. We are acutely aware that this is not merely an occasional practice, but a very common one, and we second Paul VI's warning:

> . . . it is unacceptable that citizens with abundant income from the resources and activity of their country should transfer a considerable part of this income abroad for their own advantage, without care for the manifest wrong they inflict on their country by doing this [*Populorum Progressio* 24].

Money, they say, has no nationality. In Latin America, a full-blown "international imperialism of money" (*Populorum Progressio* 26) prevails—fruit of an unbridled liberalism in our economies.

There is violence as well in the growing inequality in the distribution of national revenues. A small minority, some 5 percent of our population, amasses enormous wealth, drawing off up to as much as 30 percent of the national income, while 80 percent of the population must rest content with 40 percent of that income. In other words, less than a third of the population enjoy two thirds of the national wealth, while the remaining two thirds plus are left with a mere third (United Nations figures on the distribution of revenue in Latin America, 1971). And this situation has a tendency to deteriorate as a result of inflation, whose repercussions are felt mostly in the most marginalized sectors of the population.

Finally, violence is suffered by working people, as they are so frequently deprived of union rights and obliged to accept inadequate compensation for their labor. Here it will be in order to recall the stern admonition of Pope Leo XIII, issued nearly a hundred years ago in his encyclical *Rerum Novarum* (no. 32):

> If, driven by need or by the fear of a still greater evil, the laborer accepts inadequate conditions against his or her will simply because employer or manager imposes these conditions, this is surely to suffer violence—a violence that cries out for justice.

Violence in the Political Domain

The Latin American political climate is scarcely conducive to the political discernment Paul VI summons us to exercise in respect of our various ideologies and systems—whether it be a matter of attempting to influence economic liberalism to overmaster its social insensitivity and begin to respect our collective rights or, at the other end of the spectrum, leading socialism to have some regard for the values of "liberty, responsibility, and openness to the spiritual" (*Octogesima Adveniens* 31).

Hence Latin America's constant vulnerability to the temptation of violence. It may be a violence expressed in the stubborn choice of the "stifling materialism" of a consumer society, which, by its intrinsic logic, only leads "to greed, to the insatiable desire for more, and can make increased power a tempting objective" (*Populorum Progressio* 18). Or it may be a violence expressed as an unbridled drive to "change the system":

> There are two different sorts of violence: violence of assault and violence of defense. There are those who seek "conflict at any price," and there are those who seek "peace at any price." The price in both cases is violence. . . . We reject both brands of violence. And we call for the radical elimination, not of the enemy, surely, but of the root cause of the enmity [Chilean Bishops, "The Gospel and Peace," September 5, 1975].

We call particular attention to and especially denounce violence exercised in the name of "national security": "Security as the good of a nation is incompatible with the insecurity of the people" (Brazilian Bishops, "Christian Exigencies of a Political Order," no. 37, February 17, 1977).

> A legitimate concern for national security must not be carried to extremes, to the point of creating a mounting insecurity throughout the country. . . . The terrorism of subversion may not be answered with the terrorism of repression [Paraguayan Bishops, Declaration of June 12, 1976, no. 8].

Furthermore, the arms race casts the dark shadows of doubt and uncertainty over our lands. Indeed, this is a specter of violence that can bear Latin America no benefit. The arms race is not only a threat of violence to come but it is itself a violence already doing its dark deed in our midst. For it exacerbates a sense of nationalism that undermines efforts toward a Latin American community of nations. It arouses a nationalism that refuses to consider other peoples as sisters and brothers.

"Nationalism isolates people from their true good" (*Populorum Progressio* 62).

To boot, nationalism impoverishes our people by further limiting their already feeble resources that are so necessary for their integral development:

> [Nationalism] would be especially harmful where the weakness of national economies demands rather the pooling of efforts, of knowledge and of funds, in order to implement programmes of development and to increase commercial and cultural exchange (*Populorum Progressio* 62).

Other Manifestations of Violence

The violence of the mighty seeks to conceal its true nature. Hence its recourse to the lie. But the lie, in turn, is also insufficient to itself—and hence has need of violence. This process then spins off all manner of secondary violence that cannot be limited only to economic and political relationships. For instance, the vicious circle of violence overflows into pornography and brutality—the familiar "sex and violence" of television—and penetrates the intimacy of the family circle itself as entertainment. Violence translates into coercive birth-control programs accepted by our governments. In this way our governments countenance an intolerable interference into the life of married couples, who alone bear the primary responsibility for the procreation and upbringing of children. There is violence when a human life is snuffed out by abortion. There is violence when the dignity of women is accorded no respect— when women are denied an equal voice in the exercise of family and social responsibility or when they are reduced to the status of objects used to advertise goods and services in a consumer society.

Violence weighs especially heavy on the poor. It is the poor who are deprived of gainful employment, opportunities for education, and necessary medical attention.

Our youth, too, fall victim to violence. They suffer the violence of thought control; their ideas and aspirations are manipulated; and they are taught to accept this dogmatism and reject another one. Thought control occurs also when young people are carefully removed from all opportunity to develop and use their critical senses and when they are denied the exercise of political responsibility. In some countries the university becomes the private perquisite of a privileged elite; in others, it reflects society's malaise, swaying with the political and economic winds of the moment. When young people are deprived of an opportunity to give their lives a meaning, and when they have lost their last glimmer of hope, they fall victim to drugs and crime. We deplore these misguided expressions of youthful protestation, and we lament the futility of our young people's efforts to make a positive contribution to the changes of which our society stands so sorely in need.

The Religious Legitimation of Violence

We call the attention of our Latin American Christian communities— more forthrightly, and more urgently than ever before—to the violence done to the Word of God when the very gospel is used to exculpate and even legitimate violence. Jesus was well aware of how structures and systems oppress human beings. He attacked the most sacred structure a religious people like the Jews can know when he taught us that "the sabbath was made for man, not man for the sabbath" (Mark 2:27). Persons may not be sacrificed to legalistic observances. But Jesus brought about the liberation he proclaimed through his death and his resurrection. He paid the highest price of all, the price of his life, to set human beings free—delivering them especially from slavery to sin and thereby from the slaveries that are sin's consequence.

Thus Jesus issued no call for violent action, even to change unjust situations. Still less then did he call for violence in order to maintain and defend a situation of injustice. Accordingly, we are bound to declare that Christian values are never defended by murder, torture, or repression. Sad indeed would be those "humanistic, Christian values" that require violence for their maintenance! Such methods can never take up the defense of that life and love that have set us free by making us children of one Father as well as sisters and brothers to all humankind. "Filiation and fraternity"—the status of children of God and brothers and sisters of one another—are not maintained by force of arms. They are values lived from within a true conversion of the heart by accepting the gifts of the Lord in a spirit of poverty.

Attitudes Toward Violence

There are several different ways in which people react to the reality of violence. Some prefer simply to ignore it; they refuse to look at it. This is an area of reality they prefer to cut themselves off from by taking refuge in the artificial, narrow, and closed world of their social class and the unreal world around them. Others are willing to admit the fact of violence but take a fatalistic view of it, as if it were an inevitable concomitant of the human condition or even a "necessary evil." For this reason violence is seen as a choice falling within the legitimate purview of discretionary human options.

In its victims violence generates passivity, resignation, and fear. When we have arrived at a society of numb masses—faceless and mute, stripped of all critical sense, deprived of human solidarity, broken and tamed by a consumer society—then violence has fully attained its objectives. This is the response to violence of those who do not believe that any action, even nonviolent action, can be of any use. Such people have capitulated to the triumph of oppressive and repressive violence, which they see as having the last word in history.

Others, however, feel themselves called to rebellion and combat. Refusing to accept our unjust world, they dream of a more just society. But they think that their utopia can be realized only through recourse to violence. Faced with the existence of "situations whose injustice cries to heaven," they have "recourse to violence, as a means to right these wrongs to human dignity" (*Populorum Progressio* 30). But the tactics of counterviolence have only led to a still greater deprivation and an even more implacable repression than before.

Nonviolent Action

The problem of violence that we have just denounced, which seems so far from finding any short-term solution, looms before us today as a challenge. We are confronted with various responses—passivity and conformism or rebellion and violent protest. Have we an alternative solution? Can we propose another way to fight against the violence of the mighty who are reducing the weak to slavery? What means of combat can we recommend to prevent the struggle of the oppressed against injustices that crush them from escalating in a wild spiral of hatred and terror?

Our meeting here in Bogotá has helped us come to see nonviolence as a mighty opportunity for Christians today and all men and women of goodwill. Now they have a way to strike a blow for a society whose goal will be victory over all forms of domination.

Nonviolent action is a spirit and a method. We are already in possession of examples of its effectiveness in various situations of injustice. Gandhi was an apostle of nonviolence in South Africa, and then in India. It was his way of fighting for liberation from colonialism and for social and political justice. Martin Luther King, Jr., became a martyr of nonviolence as he struggled to defend the black victims of discrimination and racial prejudice. Danilo Dolci battled for the liberation of the poverty-stricken masses of Sicily from the terrorism of the Mafia. César Chávez organized the exploited Chicanos of the California vineyards and lettuce fields and continues his nonviolent struggle at their side today. Nonviolence was used in Czechoslovakia against the Russian invasion.

These examples may seem far removed or hard to adapt to the Latin American reality. And yet partisans of the nonviolent cause are rising up among us as well. Dom Hélder Câmara is one of its pioneers in Latin America. Nor is he alone: We are overjoyed to see that the masses of the people, especially the poor and the oppressed, already possess in some of their leaders and pastoral ministers inspiring examples of nonviolent, evangelical activity against injustice and oppression. Latin America already has its lists of martyrs and confessors of nonviolence.

But we must also recognize that we Christians have not always denounced violence and injustice. In our weakness and sin we have sometimes even gone so far as to furnish a counterwitness by our connivance with oppressors of the poor and perpetrators of injustice.

The Spirit of Nonviolence

Nonviolent action is the concretization of a spirit and a method. As a spirit, nonviolence takes its point of departure in the conviction that human beings are not irremediably set in mutual confrontation as enemies—that even in the midst of conflict they can always accept the challenge to transcend that conflict through dialogue and love. When conflict springs from an evident situation of injustice characterized by the predominance of the power of some persons over others, the weak have the task of undertaking an act of moral pressure. This act needs to be extremely energetic and telling but nonviolent. Its aim should be to reveal to their oppressors their own injustice and to influence them to correct it. In this way both sides break free—the strong from the oppression they are inflicting and the weak from the oppression they have been suffering.

To be sure, the spirit of nonviolence is not a Christian monopoly. Still we do find in our faith and in the words and actions of the Lord Jesus a profound motivation and clear examples of nonviolent action in real life. In Christianity, then, such action is the incarnation of a way of living the gospel by coming to grips with the injustices of this world.

Hence nonviolence must begin with the radical transformation of our personal lives. We must do violence to ourselves—we need to transcend the selfish instincts that divide us among ourselves and cut us off from our sisters and brothers. We have to conquer the temptation to accommodation and passivity by overcoming the fear that grips our hearts. We must uproot all the seeds of hatred, resentment, and vengeance that may have sprouted up within us and that express themselves in our immediate interpersonal relationships. Nonviolence is a response to violence and oppression; only it is not a response in kind. It is not the product of an instinctual mechanism that will determinedly mete out measure for measure. It is a response welling up out of the deepest reaches of our interior liberty, giving us the capacity to repair human relationships by restoring a respect for personhood and freedom. The spirit of reconciliation never springs from cowardice or weakness. Christian forgiveness is the fruit of love and an act of freedom. It creates freedom in others.

We find the clearest example of the spirit of nonviolence in dialogue. We know how difficult it is to have a dialogue while it is easy to have two simultaneous monologues. In a monologue we seek to justify ourselves alone and to denounce the errors of our adversary alone. In a dialogue, on the other hand, we begin by seeking the truth that lies with the other side, the good there is in our adversary. We have to be honest enough to tell him or her what we have found. Next, dialogue requires us to raise our consciousness of the manner in which we ourselves in our lives have betrayed the truth we find in our adversary. Only then may we declare our own truth—in full knowledge that we have often been unfaithful to it, too, by our actions.

Finally—having completed the first three steps—we may proceed to the fourth. Now we may declare to our adversary the wrong we find in him or her, the injustice he or she is committing. But the manner of our declaration must be such as to engage our adversary to join us in a companionable journey up the road to justice, as we confess that all of us are sinners. Thus in a dialogue that is sincere, the liberating word is pronounced—the word that delivers not only us but also our adversary as well from the oppression of the evil within us all.

To set out on the road of nonviolence means making a distinction between the wrong committed by the oppressor and his or her personhood. One must love the person and hate the evil. This is why nonviolent action may never have recourse to force and power. Indeed, it may never offend the oppressor by so much as an insulting word. On the contrary, in imitation of Christ, nonviolent persons will endeavor to live the spirituality of the Suffering Servant of Isaiah 53. They will avoid all spirit of domination over other human beings. They will eschew all signs of discrimination or superiority. They will seek serenity by means of an ongoing program of training in order to overcome their fear. They will live in truth, they will tell the truth, and they will defend the truth—but always with love.

Commitment to the spirit and mystique of nonviolence means taking up the challenge of following Jesus, all the way to his seeming human failure. For that failure became the seed of humanity's radical transformation. It is love, not violence or hatred, that will have the last word in history. Jesus' resurrection delivers us from the seeming absurdity of a meaningless death when we are crushed by the mighty ones of this world. His resurrection is the proclamation of a community of sisters and brothers among all men and women. For we are all children of the same Father who is in heaven.

The Method of Nonviolence

Nonviolence is lived in concrete action. As action, it has a relationship to the social reality, and thereby to all the power of institutionalized violence within that reality. It neither ignores nor camouflages that violence. Least of all does it admit its legitimation as necessary and inevitable. On the contrary, it forthrightly denounces violence as an optional product of the human mind and heart, the fruit of human beings' free decisions, choices, and preferences. Nonviolence is not to be confused with passivity, inertia, or the toleration of injustice.

Like all human activity, in order to be efficacious nonviolence must be persevering, clear in its objectives, and methodical in its procedure. Far from rejecting the mediation of social analysis, it considers such an analysis indispensable for discerning the real problems—for identifying concrete injustices along with their causes and deep mutual bonds. Nonviolent action intends to provoke changes in history. Its view of the human being and society stimulate it to use methods and acts of non cooperation against unjust economic, political, and technological systems. As these acts of collective moral pressure mount up and accumulate, they begin gradually and systematically to withdraw all these unjust systems' support. And they compel the discovery and construction—from its foundations to its pinnacle—of an alternative, socialized society.

Nonviolent action implants, by anticipation within the very process of change itself, the values to which the change will ultimately lead. Hence it does not sow peace by means of war. It does not attempt to build up by tearing down; neither does it contradict its own aspirations for a community of brothers and sisters by the very acts through which it seeks to transform society.

Nonviolent action perseveres. It is nourished by the conviction that the human person is of absolute worth. Our Christian faith gives to this conviction a powerful impetus. For we believe in the person and work of Jesus, the nonviolent One par excellence. If we compare nonviolent action with Marxism, we observe at once that both approaches strive to rise above the conflicts of a class society. But when this kind of concept closes itself off from transcendence, it condemns humanity to an alienation from itself. Without the presence of the living God, it is impossible to surmount the inevitable contradictions of the human condition and to break free of the psychosocial conditioning that alienates us from our innate freedom. The root of the absolute value of human personhood lies in its openness to the transcendent God, in its spontaneous inclination to conduct a dialogue with him.

Lines of Action

A good deal of the work of our meeting here in Bogotá consisted of reflections and discussions in small groups. We now wish to present some of the specific reflections generated in these groups. Our discussions centered on three themes. Without pretending that these themes exhaust the problems and challenges of nonviolence, we shall present our conclusions just as our groups stated them when we came together at the final session of the meeting. Of course, we recognize that we have not had the time to examine and discuss fully and maturely all the ramifications of these themes. Nevertheless, the majority of the participants thought it would be useful to set forth the results of our reflections as a basis for further exploration. For they reflect the living situation in numerous regions of Latin America. The church may not neglect to propose answers to these problems, however tentative they may be.

We considered the following topics: (1) the problems of the peasantry, especially problems concerned with ownership of the land; (2) national security regimes; and (3) conflicts in the church, especially in the area of nonviolent action for justice.

Land Problems

We cannot analyze here the manifold problems of the peasant class. Still less can we undertake to indicate a solution for each of these problems. Nevertheless, we wish to reiterate our conviction that the free, active, and responsible participation of the peasants is an indispensable condition for the attainment of just solutions.

Our pastoral enterprise among the peasants must spring from a life in their midst—from a prayerful reflection that will bring problems to light and allow the whole of our lives to be illumined by the light of the gospel. We must be witnesses of the conviction and trust that "prayer and fasting" (Matt. 17:21) has power to move hearts and mobilize action.

Our pastoral work must encourage the participation of the peasantry not only in the basic Christian communities but also in unions and peasant organizations. It is not our pastoral task to organize lay groups directly. But it is our duty to prepare and encourage lay persons to undertake this role.

All our activity must imply a respect for persons and hence a respect for the initiatives people may take in their expressions of piety, including liturgical expressions and the launching of new ministries. We should demonstrate this same respect as the peasants take the initiative in defending their right to the land.

And yet there are cases where the only available voice of those who have no voice is the church. In such cases, if the cause of the peasants is just, and if they request our intervention, we may act as mediators or even take up their actual defense. At times, this will mean opposition to the might of the oligarchies that concentrate in their hands all power of decision. And it will always mean discharging the mission of prophet toward government authorities and public opinion by taking up the defense of the peasants' rights as well as toward the peasants themselves by making them aware of these rights.

The National Security Regimes

Amid the situations of violence from which Latin America suffers, there have arisen in various countries new political regimes that are authoritarian in nature. Often they have been established by the armed forces. These regimes hold themselves out as the necessary solution and remedy for problems of violence. We applaud the intention of these regimes to make an end of acts of institutionalized violence. But in our view the means employed to remedy these evils calls for certain correctives.

Generally the methods employed pose the problem of attempting to combat violence with violence, so that the spiral of violence escalates indefinitely. Repression of violence by a regime that itself uses violent methods increases rather than diminishes violence. This method of attempting to establish security becomes a vicious circle, and thus only leads to insecurity rather than national security. Thus violence on the part of the opposition engenders insecurity on the part of the state. The state, in turn, sows insecurity among the citizenry by its own measures of violence and repression. The insecurity of the population sparks more state violence, which inspires still more popular insecurity. When the state responds with new repression, an endless spiral is under way. Someone among the parties must take it upon himself or herself to break the vicious circle of insecurity/violence.

1. The national security regimes attempt to justify their violence first of all by an appeal to the fight against terrorism. To be sure, we reject a priori and absolutely any and every act of terrorism and violence. We accord such acts no value whatever in the struggle for social justice. Furthermore, we recognize the right and duty of the state to suppress acts of terrorism, kidnappings, the commandeering of aircraft, and the like, including the obligation to prevent their repetition in so far as this is possible by morally acceptable means.

Nevertheless, we think that in a good many cases all proportion has been lacking between the actual extent of terrorist activity and the response of national security states. Such states react as if the nation's very survival were at stake—as if the country were on the brink of total destruction by war. This is an overreaction. There is no proportion between acts of subversion that are committed and an across-the-board suppression of every form of civil and human rights. The climate of insecurity generated by the very measures that are intended to guarantee security is abundant evidence of this fact. In no instance is the survival of any nation or state really in jeopardy. Of course, even if this were so, this would not justify recourse to inhumane means to assure the state's survival. State and nation are not absolute ends but intermediate ones; they are subordinate to the absolutely inalienable rights of the human person.

Very often the methods used to suppress terrorism are themselves terrorist methods. It is a matter of record that in some regimes the police, with the tacit complicity of the authorities, are actually setting up their own terrorist groups in the form of Death Squads.

Furthermore, the national security regimes artificially pad their lists of terrorists and subversives by simply including all advocates of any form of criticism or political opposition. All who practice even the most peaceful, nonviolent means of opposition to the political programs of the government, all who have any reservations about these programs, and even all who are indifferent to them and neglect to demonstrate the required enthusiasm for the actions of the government—all such persons are labeled subversives. Thus the state can list artificially large numbers of dangerous and violent enemies.

Furthermore, the simple repression of subversion can never be a lasting remedy, for it fails to take account of the causes of subversion. Most of these causes reside in our situations of institutionalized violence. Thus the radical remedy for subversion is the radical suppression of social inequalities and the cessation of assaults on and infringements of individual, social, and political liberties.

2. The national security regimes appeal to the need to defend the nation against communism or international Marxism. They represent the situation as if their countries were on the verge of falling into the hands of the Soviet Union and becoming people's democracies on the model of the communist countries.

Here again, we have to wonder whether we are not dealing with an exaggerated assessment of the danger. Serious observers in the world of international public opinion fail to recognize any substance in these fears, at least at the present time. No proportion appears between the actual danger of the establishment of a communist regime and the repressive measures currently applied in the form of the suppression of human rights.

And here as well, the national security regimes, through their propaganda organizations, multiply the number of communists beyond all bounds. They find communists everywhere, even where none exist. They treat anyone who denounces a situation of injustice or takes up the defense of the poor as a communist. When groups the world over plead for human rights, they call it an international communist campaign. They even go so far as to label as communist infiltrators any bishop, priest, or Christian lay person who denounces their vicious assaults on human rights or dares call attention to the pitiful situation of the masses fallen in sacrifice to the prevailing social systems.

Moreover, in their zeal for total security and radical repression, the National Security systems find themselves obliged to combat communism by the very weapons and immoral methods they denounce in the communists themselves. Thus their anticommunist crusade loses all moral legitimacy.

We must also observe that the purely repressive methods by which the national security regimes endeavor to eradicate communism actually have the effect of enhancing the prestige of communism with the oppressed and terrorized masses. The experience of other countries confirms the fact that like methods of combating communism actually promote it and confer on its devotees the halo of martyrs. There are methods of battling communism that seem calculated precisely to pave the way for it.

3. The national security regimes appeal to the failure of democracy. We grant, to be sure, that the democratic methods of nonviolence and dialogue would have proved more effective had they corrected certain of their shortcomings. But instead of merely correcting the shortcomings, the new regimes insist on breaking with the past and obliterating the progress made in the course of the democratic experiments.

They suspend their own constitutions and suppress their own political and social institutions. What they should have done is to amend and correct them. Instead, they pretend that they have definitively demonstrated the ineffectiveness of these institutions. Popular participation in the process of government, they aver, has proved sterile and unproductive. Only a state in the hands of a special elite can work. But here again, there is no proportion between the actual evils and the draconian remedies proposed. Have we not had to suffer failings in our systems of popular representation? Then let us suppress all popular representation. Or so our leaders seem to reason.

They are only preparing a new democracy, they assure us. We are overjoyed to hear this declaration of intent. But then why do they so assiduously avoid any appearance of the civic education that might prepare the people for some participation in the affairs of state? Why do they disparage representative institutions, oppose any critical study of the prevailing situation, and reject proposed remedies out of hand? How can they hope to have popular participation in the governmental process by simple authoritarian decree?

4. Finally, the national security regimes appeal to their successes in the economic domain. No matter the totalitarian, authoritarian character of their modes of development—their gains in this area are presented as adequate justification for the existence of these regimes.

Now no one is more earnestly desirous of development than we ourselves. Furthermore, we are altogether well aware that no development can be conceived of that would not entail great sacrifices on the part of the population. Nevertheless, we cannot entertain the claim that material gains of an economic kind are worth the price of institutionalized political violence, government by surveillance, a secret police, the elimination of popular representation in the political process, and the total abrogation of individual liberties. Such a state of violence can never be justified on grounds of tangible results in the shape of quantitative economic gains. More preferable would be a slower rate of economic progress with less violence and more liberty.

Furthermore, the economic progress itself is not without its serious questions. We hear of a Brazilian economic miracle that other states are so anxious to reproduce that they sometimes announce a like "miracle," even when there is nothing of the kind. But for whom is this economic miracle a miracle? For a small social category that has reaped its total benefit, while the great masses of the poverty-stricken find themselves even poorer than they were before. That is to say, the price of this miracle in the last analysis is but another form of domination, still more sacrifices imposed on the poor, and more economic violence, via political violence, to the sole advantage of a few privileged persons. Is this the justification for the violent methods of the state?

Indeed, a good many commentators question whether the economic gains claimed by these authoritarian regimes are, in fact, the result of these regimes and their special methods. They hold that the same results would have been obtained in a democratic system—with correctives, to be sure, but without totalitarian distortions.

In a word, we remain unconvinced by the arguments brought forward in justification of a regime of repression and violence. We by no means wish to oppose these regimes by another form of violence. On the contrary, we feel the moment has come to shatter the vicious circle of violence and oppose these systems by means of a determined, persevering action without violence—forthright and clearly defined, on the order of active noncooperation—with a view to totally transforming the structures of political and economic violence prevailing in our countries.

Conflicts Within the Church and Nonviolent Action for Justice

There is no hiding the fact that there are conflicts within the Latin American church. They are there for all to see, and the media dutifully report them to public opinion—if not always without distorting them. We must face these conflicts for what they are, come to understand them, and strive to overcome them. But that unity or reconciliation would be unevangelical indeed which were to be attained by stifling dissent, by ignoring the causes of the dissent, or by compromises to be reached only at the price of a spirit of resignation and the mutual abandonment of convictions or forms of activity felt to have come from the inspiration of the Spirit. We seek reconciliation, not a betrayal of the world we should be serving and saving. We seek reconciliation by the transcendence of our divisions, not by their negation or by the denial of both them and their causes.

First, we recognize that divergencies and divisions do arise over the nonviolent action undertaken in the cause of justice and peace here in Latin America, at the heart of our conflicts today. Thus it is we ourselves who are provoking some of these divisions, however much we may wish to do the very opposite. We accept the consequences of our attitude. Our nonviolent action on behalf of peace and justice flows from the new awareness we have of the reality of the situation in which our people are living. But we who appreciate this situation of violence in our countries are in the minority. We have this appreciation in virtue of certain privileged experiences we have had. There are differences between our perception of reality and that of others. There are differences between our perception of the urgent pastoral priorities and others' estimation of these priorities. We believe that these differences are due essentially to differences in the perception of today's world—different views of what the real dangers are, what the urgent challenges are, what the real hopes and fears and sufferings of our people are, and what these people expect from the church.

But beyond these differences in the perception of worldly reality, there are sometimes differences of another kind as well: differences concerning the role of the church in the world. Per se, these are theological differences. But theological approaches, more often than not, are themselves conditioned by particular views of the reality of the world around us.

This being the case, the price of unity may never be a refusal to admit that we see what we see or know what we know. Our view may be partial, and our manner of action may seem aggressive to some of our brothers and sisters. The conflicts we shall be having to face within the church will aid us to correct and improve our view of reality and even our nonviolent action itself. As a result, we may be able to transform our action—not by renouncing the light we have received, to be sure, but by receiving other light from our sisters and brothers.

Realism obliges us to accept the objections and admonitions our brothers and sisters may offer us if they think our attitudes call for such an action. But we find it sad that some, instead of being willing to enter into a dialogue, engage in public denunciations without proof and even without any real evidence of lay persons, priests, and bishops as communist subversives and extremists. Such denunciations may be based entirely on a false interpretation of these persons' conduct, which others may find hard to understand but which they have no right to distort. In Brazil, Ecuador, Argentina, and El Salvador, priests, bishops, and especially lay persons, have recently fallen victim to repression as a result of being denounced by their fellow Christians. Brother has delivered up brother and sister betrayed sister to the violence of a repressive system.

We do not believe that public denunciations to the Holy See or other ecclesiastical authorities are an appropriate means for the attainment of church unity. This would be a unity based on the physical or moral elimination of all who seek honestly to engage in the nonviolent struggle for justice. Surely we are prepared to suffer persecution as a consequence of our nonviolent action. But we confess that persecution at the hands of our own brothers and sisters is particularly painful.

We cannot ignore the fact that certain divisions in the church are the reflection of the divisions occasioned by Jesus' own mission on earth. For, as he himself declares, he has come to spread division (cf. Matt. 10:34–35). True, Jesus is for everyone, and his message is addressed to all. But he does not address all in the same fashion. For example, the words he speaks to the poor are different from those he speaks to the rich. His gospel does not have the same resonance, the same meaning, for the rich as for the poor. The words he addresses to the poor are filled with hope and gladness. The words he addresses to the rich are charged with deep concern and with appeals for conversion, the abandonment of special privileges, and active compassion in the distribution of the goods of this world. What Jesus says to the poor always tends to arouse joy and gratitude, even if it fails actually to do so in individual cases. What he says to the rich often provokes wrath and persecution. Our evangelization should be based on the same approach—otherwise it will not be an evangelization according to the gospel of Jesus Christ.

We cannot agree with those of our brothers and sisters who seek to reduce the gospel to a message of false universality—bland tidings to all in the same tone that blissfully washes out the differences between rich and poor and speaks as if there is no difference between a rich Christian and a poor Christian. Such an insipid gospel can never be the leaven of resolute action for justice and the liberation of our people.

We cannot resign ourselves to a church unity based on an abstract universality, on a colorless, odorless, and tasteless gospel of equality among all human beings that takes no account of social, economic, and cultural differences. Our love for the unity of the church must drive us forward together in search of a full gospel, a gospel read in its totality—not a mawkish message in which all differences vanish into thin air. The price of unity may never be the sacrifice of our option for the poor by ignoring their existence in our preaching and practice. This kind of unity would be the very contrary of the eschatological unity in fullness for which Jesus prayed. For we do not seek the peace the world gives, but the peace of Jesus (cf. John 14:27), which is the fruit of the effort of all the generations of apostles down through the ages toward the day when the kingdom of God will be finally fulfilled.

Appendix B

Acceptance Speech of Adolfo Pérez Esquivel on the Occasion of the Presentation of the Nobel Prize for Peace in 1980

Your Majesty,
Mr. President of the Nobel Committee,
Committee members,
Ladies and Gentlemen:

With humility I stand before you to receive the high distinction that the Nobel Committee and the Parliament grant to those who have committed their lives on behalf of peace and to the pursuit of justice and solidarity among nations.

I want to receive this distinction in the name of the people of Latin America and, in a very special way, in the name of the poorest and smallest of my brothers and sisters because they are the most beloved of God. I receive it in the name of my indigenous brothers and sisters, the peasants, workers, and young people—in the name of the thousands of members of religious orders and of men and women of goodwill who relinquish their privileges to share the life and path of the poor, and who struggle to build a new society.

For a man like myself—a small voice for those who have no voice— who struggles so that the cry of the people may be heard in all its power; for one without any identifying affiliation other than as a flesh-and-blood Latin American and as a Christian, this is, without any doubt, the highest honor that I can receive, which is to be considered a servant of peace.

I come from a continent that lives between anguish and hope. For this continent where I live, the choice of the evangelical power of nonviolence presents itself, I am convinced, as a challenge that opens up new and radical perspectives.

It is a choice that gives priority to a value essentially and profoundly Christian—the dignity of the human being, the sacred, transcendent, and irrevocable dignity that belongs to the human being by reason of being a child of God and a brother or sister in Christ, and therefore our own brother or sister.

In these long years of struggle for our organization—the Service for Peace and Justice in Latin America—we have walked by the side of the poorest and most disadvantaged.

We don't have much to say but, we do have much to share in order to achieve, by means of the nonviolent struggle, the abolition of injustices and the attainment of a more just and humane society for all.

It is a walking side by side with our brothers and sisters—with those who are persecuted, those who hunger and thirst for justice, those who suffer because of oppression, those who are anguished by the prospect of war, those who suffer the cruel impact of violence or see constantly postponed the achievement of their basic rights. It is for all of them that I am here today.

My voice would like to have the strength of the voice of the humble and lowly. It is a voice that denounces injustice and proclaims hope in God and humanity. For this hope is the hope of all human beings who yearn to live in communion with all persons as their brothers and sisters and as children of God.

Latin America is a young, vibrant region of the earth, which was described by Pope Paul VI as a region of hope.

To really understand this means to discern and grasp a reality with the clear-cut task of sharing in its destiny. To understand this means to achieve a profound identification with the people who are the protagonists in this historical process, and who are willing to transform pain and suffering by love, thus assuming in this perspective the praxis of Jesus.

When we look at the world our people live in, we see what is an affront to God. For millions of children, young people, adults, and elderly persons live under the sign and mark of underdevelopment.

The institutionalized violence, the poverty and the oppression generate a dual reality—the result of the maintenance of political and economic systems that create injustice and sanctify a social order that benefits only a few. The reality is that the rich become increasingly richer at the expense of the poor who become increasingly poorer.

In the face of that grim truth—like the Catholic bishops in Puebla, like the Christians committed to the movements that struggle for human rights, like all persons of goodwill—I want to share the anguish that appears on the suffering faces of the Latin American man or woman in whom we see the suffering face of Christ, Our Lord, who confronts and challenges us.

As I speak to you, I have before my eyes the vivid recollection of the faces of my brothers and sisters:

—the faces of workers and peasants living at subhuman levels, whose rights to organize are severely limited;

—the faces of children suffering from malnutrition;

—the faces of young people who see their hopes frustrated;

—the faces of outcast and marginal urban poor;

—the faces of the indigenous peoples;

—the faces of the mothers searching for their missing sons and daughters;

—the faces of those who have disappeared, many of them just children;

—the faces of thousands of exiles;

—the faces of people who lay claim to liberty and justice for all.

Despite so much suffering and pain, I live in hope because I feel that Latin America has risen to its feet. Its liberation can be delayed but never denied.

We live in hope because we believe, like St. Paul, that love never dies. Human beings in the historical process have created enclaves of love by their active practice of solidarity throughout the world, and with a view to the full-orbed liberation of peoples and all humanity.

For me it is essential to have the inward peace and serenity of prayer in order to listen to the silence of God, which speaks to us, in our personal lives and in the history of our times, about power of love.

Because of our faith in Christ and humankind, we must apply our humble efforts to the construction of a more just and humane world. And I want to declare emphatically: *Such a world is possible.*

To create this new society, we must present outstretched and friendly hands, without hatred and rancor, even as we show great determination and never waver in the defense of truth and justice. Because we know that we cannot sow seeds with clenched fists. To sow we must open our hands.

I want to express my thanks to all of you and to the Nobel Committee for this high distinction bestowed on the humble people of Latin America.

I am deeply moved and at the same time more committed to redouble my efforts in the struggle for peace and justice. We know that peace is only possible when it is the fruit of justice. True Peace is the result of the profound transformation effected by nonviolence which is, indeed, the power of love.

I should tell you that, thanks to the support and understanding of my wife and children, even in the hardest and most difficult moments of the struggle I was able to press forward, together with my brothers and sisters of Latin America. With their love, silence, and solidarity they have always helped to strengthen me and give me the courage to serve my brothers and sisters.

Invoking the strength of Christ, Our Lord, I want to share with you, with my people, and with the world what he taught us in the Sermon on the Mount:

> How happy are the poor in spirit;
> theirs is the kingdom of heaven.
> Happy the gentle:
> they shall have the earth for their heritage.
> Happy those who mourn:
> they shall be comforted.
> Happy those who hunger and thirst for what is right:
> they shall be satisfied.
> Happy the merciful:
> they shall have mercy shown them.
> Happy the pure in heart:
> they shall see God.
> Happy the peacemakers:
> they shall be called sons of God.
> Happy those who are persecuted in the cause of right:
> theirs is the kingdom of heaven.
> Happy are you when people abuse you and persecute you and speak all kinds of calumny against you on my account. Rejoice and be glad, for your reward will be great in heaven; this is how they persecuted the prophets before you.

[Matt. 3–12].

Accept my profound gratitude and my wish for peace and well-being.

Adolfo Pérez Esquivel

Oslo
December 10, 1980

Notes

Introduction

1. Document Dial D 642, September 4, 1980. Cf. *Le Monde diplomatique,* October 1980.
2. Official statement by the government of Argentina.

Part One The Elephant and the Ant:
The Voice of Adolfo Pérez Esquivel

1. The Peace and Justice Service proposes three steps for nonviolent action: (1) Identify the injustice and call it directly to the attention of the competent authority; (2) if the dialogue with the authority fails, involve the masses of the people through public fasts and appeals to public opinion, but without causing spontaneous acts that only indicate a stymied maneuver; and (3) if such measures fail as well, then call for civil disobedience. In this connection Pérez Esquivel clings to the deeper meaning of nonviolence.
2. John Eagleson and Philip Scharper, eds., *Puebla and Beyond: Documentation and Commentary* (Maryknoll, N.Y.: Orbis Books, 1979), p. 128.

Part Two Testimonials of Nonviolence

1. The Trilateral Commission is an international task force established on the initiative of David Rockefeller; its members are leading economic and political figures from the United States, Europe, and Japan.
2. An allusion is made here to Che Guevara's guerilla strategy.
3. *Ultimas Noticias,* September 27, 1974.
4. *O Trabalhador Rural,* nos. 9–12, September/December 1977, pp. 8–9.
5. Ibid., p. 10.
6. St. Irenaeus of Lyons, *Adversus Haereses* 2.
7. The Agrarian Leagues of Paraguay were accused by an Argentine newspaper of having ties to the guerilla forces in Argentina. The accusation was then picked up by the media in Paraguay. The Agrarian Leagues easily proved the falsehood of the report, which was allegedly based on information furnished by the leagues themselves. The report was a forgery, probably of Paraguayan origin.